**Assessing Children in Need and their Families:**

Practice Guidance

*Department of Health*

# Assessing Children in Need and their Families:

## Practice Guidance

*London*

*The Stationery Office*

## Social Care Group

The Social Care Group is one of the four business groups in the Department of Health. It is jointly headed by the Chief Social Services Inspector and the Head of Social Care Policy. It supports Ministers in promoting high quality, cost effective services through

- national policies
- support to external social care agencies
- inspection

The Social Services Inspectorate is a part of the Social Care Group. It is headed by the Chief Social Services Inspector who is the principal professional advisor to Ministers on social services and related matters.

## Web Access

This document is available on the DoH internet web site at:
http://www.open.gov.uk/doh/quality.htm

This publication is also available on The Stationery Office website at
https://www.the-stationery-office.co.uk/doh/pgacn/pgacn.htm

The Stationery Office site contains the document in a fully searchable format together with links to related publications referenced in the text. The data is held on a secure site that is password protected so you will need the following information to access it:
*User name:* pgacneed
*Password:* r5ch8rd
Please note that both fields are case sensitive and contain no spaces.

First published 2000
Second impression 2000

ISBN 0 11 322418 4

Printed in the United Kingdom for The Stationery Office.
TJ003127   c40   12/00   (6157)

# Contents

# Foreword

This publication is a companion volume to the Guidance on the *Framework for the Assessment of Children in Need and their Families*. It is a significant contribution to a major programme of work led by the Department of Health to provide guidance, practice materials and training resources on assessing children in need and their families. This is to assist in the achievement of one of the government's key policy objectives in children's services, delivered through the Quality Protects Programme, to ensure that referral and assessment processes discriminate effectively between different types and level of need, and produce a timely response.

Whilst government policy objectives may be clear, effective implementation requires detailed knowledge and understanding. The practice guidance has been produced to help policy makers, managers and practitioners who have responsibility for responding to the needs of some of our most disadvantaged and vulnerable children. The needs of some children require particular knowledge and sensitivity to ensure they do not suffer further disadvantage. These include children from black and minority ethnic families and disabled children. The issues involved in assessing their needs within the context of their families and communities are discussed by leading professionals in their field. The steering and advisory groups, which were set up to develop the Guidance on the Assessment Framework, have contributed to these perspectives.

It is hoped this publication will be a valuable resource for use in promoting evidence-based practice, not only in direct work with children and families but also in training and continuing staff development.

John Hutton

John Hutton
MINISTER OF STATE FOR SOCIAL SERVICES

*March 2000*

# Introduction

> The body of knowledge available to those who struggle with today's problems of child care is still rudimentary compared with the physical sciences; but it is by far and away greater than what could called upon in the past... Indeed, social work today is expected to be 'evidence-based', something that would have been an unrealistic aspiration in, say, the 1950s, when there was virtually no evidence upon which to draw (Parker, 1999, pp.54–55).

Understanding what is happening to a child when there are concerns that the child's health and development are being impaired remains a core professional activity for those working with children and families. The knowledge which is available to assist them has expanded dramatically over the last two decades. However, it has not always been easily available to practitioners and their managers. The development of the *Framework for the Assessment of Children in Need and their Families* (jointly issued by the Department of Health, the Department for Education and Employment and the Home Office, 2000) has drawn heavily, from many disciplines, on the wealth of research and accumulated practice experience about the developmental needs of children. The aim of the practice guidance in this accompanying publication is to make transparent the evidence base for the Assessment Framework, thereby assisting professionals in their tasks of analysis, judgement and decision making.

Chapter 1 highlights some of the key theories, research findings and practice wisdom which have underpinned the development of the Assessment Framework and in which confidence can be placed. Staff who are working with children and families may find further exploration of the texts referenced in this chapter helpful in informing their practice. Chapter 2 provides more specific knowledge and guidance about working with black children and their families and points to useful sources of information. Chapter 3 similarly provides knowledge and guidance about assessing the needs of disabled children and their families. These two chapters address issues of major importance which must be integral to policy, planning, management and practice in work with children and families. However, the messages which can be drawn from these two chapters can be used in work with **all** children.

The Department of Health is grateful to the authors of the chapters:

Chapter 1: Wendy Rose, Senior Research Fellow and Jane Aldgate, Professor of
　　　　　　Social Care, The Open University

Chapter 2: Ratna Dutt OBE, Director, REU and Melanie Phillips, Researcher, Trainer and Consultant to REU

Chapter 3: Ruth Marchant and Mary Jones, Directors of Triangle

The concluding chapter, Chapter 4, outlines a significant package of Department of Health commissioned resources which can be used to support staff in their practice and in their professional development. These resources include texts summarising key messages from relevant research findings, questionnaires and scales to assist work with children and families, training materials and other work under development.

These are only a selection of what is available. Knowledge is continually being updated and important developments will take place over the next few years. It is, therefore, incumbent on all professionals involved in training, management and practice to be continually alert to new resources, to ensure that work with children and families is firmly evidence-based. Through the Department of Health's Quality Protects Programme, an important process of change is underway aimed at improving the outcomes for children in need. The development of the *Framework for the Assessment of Children in Need and their Families* and its associated materials forms a significant part of this programme.

Jenny Gray

SOCIAL CARE GROUP
DEPARTMENT OF HEALTH

REFERENCES

Department of Health, Department for Education and Employment and Home Office (2000) *Framework for the Assessment of Children in Need and their Families*. Stationery Office, London.

Holman B, Parker R and Utting W (1999) *Reshaping Child Care Practice*. NISW, London.

# 1

## Knowledge underpinning the Assessment Framework

### What is meant by knowledge in this chapter

1.1 Throughout the *Framework for the Assessment of Children in Need and their Families* (Department of Health et al, 2000) to which this practice guidance relates, it has been emphasised that the framework is grounded in knowledge. Knowledge is defined as theory, research findings and practice experience in which confidence can be placed to assist in the gathering of information, its analysis and the choice of intervention in formulating the child's plan.

1.2 This chapter explores how theory, research and practice assist in understanding each of the three domains or systems of the framework and their interaction, the roles and tasks of the child and family worker, the processes of planning and decision making and the importance of evidence based work.

1.3 There are many theories from a range of disciplines which contribute to the understanding of human growth and development and the interaction between internal and external factors which have an impact on the lives of individuals. Schofield (1998, p.57) summarises the importance of the interplay of these factors which can be applied to the Assessment Framework:

> Social workers need a framework for understanding and helping children and families which takes into account the inner world of the self and the outer world of the environment, both in terms of relationships and in terms of practicalities such as housing. It is the capacity of social workers to be aware of and integrate in their practice these different areas of concern which defines the distinctive nature of their professional identity.

In Chapter 2 of the Guidance on the Assessment Framework (Department of Health et al, 2000), the three domains of child's developmental needs, parenting capacity and family and environmental factors are described (Figure 1). These domains and their interrelationship take account of 'the inner world of the self and the outer world of the environment' (Schofield, 1998).

### Child development

1.4 It has long been recognised that children develop along several dimensions, often simultaneously, and that they need to reach a series of milestones along each dimension if optimal outcomes are to be achieved. It is acknowledged that there will be differential development across the dimensions for some children, for instance,

Figure 1  **The Assessment Framework**

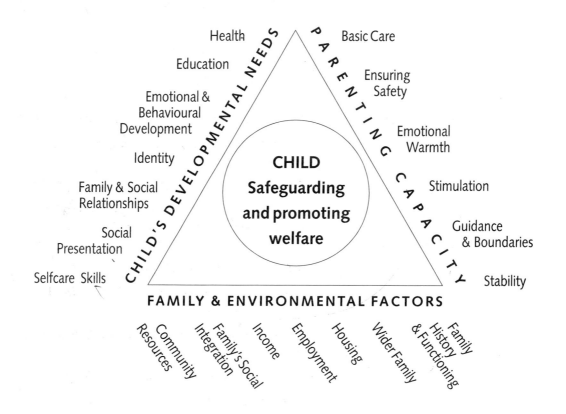

those with impairments. Different aspects of development will have more or less weight at different stages of a child's life. For example, in the early years, there is an emphasis on achieving physical milestones. Sheridan's charts on development in the early years, from one month to five years are a valuable source of reference here (Appendix 1). In middle childhood, social and academic capacity becomes more prominent although the physical development continues (for example Rushton et al, 1988), while the adolescent strives to reconcile social and emotional dependence and independence (Department of Health, 1996). Some examples of developmental tasks to be achieved at different stages are summarised by Masten and Coatsworth (1998) in Figure 2.

Figure 2 **Examples of Developmental Tasks**

| Age Period | Task |
| --- | --- |
| Infancy to preschool | Attachment to caregiver(s) |
| | Language |
| | Differentiation of self from environment |
| | Self control & compliance |
| Middle childhood | School adjustment (attendance, appropriate conduct) |
| | Academic achievement (eg. learning to read, do arithmetic) |
| | Getting along with peers (acceptance, making friends) |
| | Rule-governed conduct (following rules of society for moral behaviour and prosocial conduct) |
| Adolescence | Successful transition to secondary schooling |
| | Academic achievement (learning skills needed for higher education & work) |
| | Involvement in extracurricular activities (eg. athletics, clubs) |
| | Forming close friendships within & across gender |
| | Forming a cohesive sense of self-identity |

Masten and Coatsworth (1998)

1.5    What happens to children in the first years of life is the foundation of later development and will affect their outcomes. The significance of this must be taken into account in the assessment process. This is why secure attachments are so important in the early years. Where these attachments are absent or broken, decisions to provide children with new attachment figures must be taken as quickly as possible to avoid developmental damage. Careful distinction has to be drawn between delay which is harmful to a child's development and taking appropriate time to make good plans.

1.6　　The seven dimensions along which children develop, discussed by Ward (Horwath (ed) 2000), are influenced by many factors. Recent empirical research, for example, has suggested connections between biological and other areas of development. The development of the infant brain mirrors developmental experience in general. It is argued by Perry (1993) that the brains of developing infants react to the quality and nature of sensory information. For example, children raised with little or no experience of verbal language may have difficulties in attaining the neuro-development required for optimal speech or language. As the result of research findings, Pugh (1999) makes the point strongly:

> Environmental stress has a negative effect not only on how the brain develops, but how it functions, and underlies our capacity to make and sustain relationships.

1.7　　Additionally, as Schofield (1998) suggests, it is important to take account of the psycho-social influences on children. Clare Winnicot described in the 1960s (quoted by Schofield) how these influences relate to what takes place in children's inner and outer worlds.

## The importance of attachment

1.8　　Two major concepts critical to the interrelationship between the inner and outer worlds are attachment and self esteem. As Schofield suggests, these are interactive. One of the most influential writers on attachment has been John Bowlby whose work is still highly relevant (1958; 1969; 1973; 1980). His work has been taken forward by others such as Rutter, Ainsworth, Fahlberg, Jones and Howe. However, the process of attachment is far from simple, as Crittenden and Ainsworth (1989, p.432) suggest:

> Attachment theory is a relatively new, open-ended theory with eclectic underpinning. ... Although it began with an attempt to understand disturbed functioning of individuals who had experienced traumatic losses or early separations, it is a theory of normal development that offers explanations for some types of atypical development (Bowlby, 1969; 1973; 1980).

Pugh (1999) argues that 'attachment theory makes an important contribution to our growing understanding of the importance of social and emotional competence as the basis of self-esteem, and a key ingredient in the concept of resilience' (which is discussed later in this chapter).

1.9　　Children who are securely attached to significant adults in early childhood have been shown to be able to develop appropriate peer relationships, and cope well with problems that confront them. It is also known that children who have had good attachment experiences will be able to use these in their relationships with their own children in later life. It is because of the importance of good attachment experiences that practice concerned with helping children who have lost attachment figures places so much emphasis on providing these children with continuity of good alternative parenting experiences. Bentovim (1998) reminds practitioners that there is strong association between significant harm and insecure attachments, citing Carlson et al (1989) who found that more than 80% of significantly harmed infants had disorganised attachments compared to less that 20% in a non-maltreated comparison group.

1.10 The central place of attachment disturbance in cases of child maltreatment is also noted by Jones et al (1999) and the relationship with parents' own experiences:

> Attachment difficulties are linked with parental childhood histories of abuse and deprivation, parental personality difficulties, as well as functional illnesses such as depression. The identification of parent/child attachment difficulties has important implications for intervention, particularly in view of the outcome literature in child maltreatment, where persisting parent/child attachment difficulties combined with evidence of psychological maltreatment on follow-up is a consistent finding (Jones, 1998).

1.11 The wealth of research on attachment reinforces the importance of paying attention to attachment in assessments of all children, irrespective of their age. Teenagers who have had poor attachment experiences in their early years are particularly vulnerable, especially if they have experienced many separations and a childhood of discontinuity. Teenagers are also vulnerable if they lose good attachments in their adolescent years. Children who are joining new families, therefore, need special attention, as BAAF (1999) suggests:

> Many children will in time build positive healthy attachments in their new family, integrate their past and present experiences, and enter adulthood with a sense of stability and belonging. Yet the experience of adult adoptees reminds us that the interruption of primary connections has consequences which are potentially lifelong, and may result in a deep sense of personal loss and rejection.

1.12 Practitioners will need to integrate multi-faceted knowledge of child development into their assessments and, in particular, what is relevant from psychodynamic theory and learning theory (Seden, 2000). The development of children's inner and outer worlds can be understood within general principles of psychodynamic theory which focuses on the importance of the psychological processes at work in three key relationships: 'between self and significant other people, past and present experience, and inner and outer reality' (Brearley, 1991, pp.49–50). These ideas are important in understanding what is happening to a child.

1.13 Children's cognitive, emotional and social development go hand in hand. Children's behaviour, both adaptive and maladaptive may be learned from their experiences. Learning theory suggests behaviour that is learned can also be unlearned, with the possibilities of maladaptive behaviours being replaced with positive, pro-social behaviours. Key exponents include Skinner (1974) on operant learning, Bandura (1977) on observational learning and Seligman (1975) on learned helplessness, and Hudson (1991) among many others. Caution has to be exercised here. The results of intervention will depend on the level and scope of children's positive and negative developmental experiences and other factors.

## Protective factors and resilience

1.14 Not only are children's experiences germane to their development but other factors within individual children, such as temperament, personality and gender all influence the way they are likely to react to experiences of their families and the environment in which they are growing up. A number of writers have summarised the factors which

5

may protect children and those which may make them more vulnerable (Rutter in Haggerty et al, 1996; Jones in Adcock and White (eds), 1998; Masten and Coatsworth, 1998). An example (Table 1) is included in this chapter from *Crossing Bridges* (Falkov (ed),1998, p.72).

1.15    Children vary widely in the way they may respond to a set of circumstances. Some children may do well even in the most adverse circumstances while others appear to have little capacity to cope with small amounts of stress. It is therefore important to understand what may act as protective factors in children's lives and what may be stressors or vulnerabilities. Increasingly, interest is being shown in the concept of resilience in children (discussed by Gilligan, 2000). Rutter (1999, pp.119–120) describes resilience as:

> The phenomenon of overcoming stress or adversity. That is, put in more operational terms, there has been a relatively good outcome for someone despite their experience of situations that have been shown to carry a major risk for the development of psychopathology.

1.16    As with attachment, resilience is a broadly based concept of some complexity. This means there must be a careful analysis which focuses not just on the individual or the family but on 'the relevant stresses and adversities in their social context' (Rutter 1999, p.159). The importance of taking a broadly based approach to the assessment of children is highlighted by current ideas on protective factors. The evidence suggests strongly that children vary considerably in their responses to positive and negative experiences. Multiple protective and adverse factors may be involved at the same time. Rutter (1999, p.119) therefore suggests in summary that:

> Children vary in their vulnerability to psycho-social stress and adversity as a result of both genetic and environmental influences; that family-wide experiences tend to impinge on individual children in quite different ways; that the reduction of negative, and increase of positive, chain reactions influences the extent to which the effects of adversity persist over time; that new experiences which open up opportunities, can provide beneficial 'turning-point' effects; that although positive experiences in themselves do not exert much of a protective effect, they can be helpful if they serve to neutralise some risk factors; and that the cognitive and affective processing of experiences is likely to influence whether or not resilience develops.

1.17    These findings have led writers such as Buchanan (1999) to talk about the importance of mobilising clusters of protective factors for children even in the most unpromising situations. This constitutes an important consideration in assessment and intervention. One of the key protective factors identified by researchers is successful school experience. Furthermore, having a parent who promotes the importance of education is another vital factor (Utting, 1996):

> One of the most significant protective factors found in the backgrounds of children from disadvantaged homes whose attainment is above average is having a parent who displays a keen interest in their education.

Writers such as Jackson (1987), Cleaver (1991), Katz et al (1997), Buchanan and Hudson (1998) and Sinclair (1998) provide ample evidence of why 'any consideration of how to meet the needs of a child must include their education' (Sinclair, 1998, p.5).

**Table 1[1]  Risks/stressors and protectors/resources relevant to children**

| Risk/stressor | Factor | Protector |
|---|---|---|
| **Intrinsic** | | |
| Younger | Age | Older |
| Male | Gender | Female |
| General or specific learning disabilities, developmental disorder, lack of educational skills | Development (language and cognitive abilities) | Good cognitive and language abilities and education skills |
| Chronic physical illness/disability | Physical health | Healthy |
| Predisposition to mental disorder, or increased risk | Genetics | No adverse predisposition |
| Difficult | Temperament | Easy |
| Belonging to minority – being 'different' experience of oppression, discrimination, racism | Ethnicity | Belonging to majority group |
| **Immediate circumstances** | | |
| Discordant/distant | Parent-child relationship | Warm/mutual |
| Lax/hostile/no control Neglect, abuse | Parenting | Positive, eg. co-operation and good control, age-appropriate interactions |
| Distant/discordant/violent | Inter-parental relationship | Mutually supportive/co-operative |
| Comorbidity, both parents ill, single parent ill | Parental mental health | Partner well |
| Absent/discordant/oppressive | Sibling and peer relationships | Warm/supportive |
| Material hardship | Socio-economic resources | Financially secure |
| Crowded, unhygenic | Housing | Good, spacious |
| Poor ethos, low support, bullying, punitive | School | Good ethos, supportive |
| Absent supports, anti-social influences | Community | Support, provision of child activities |
| **Life events** | | |
| Loss and other negative life events and experiences | Life events and experiences | Positive life events, acknowledgement of achievements |

1. Reproduced with kind permission of the authors. From: Falkov A (ed) ( 1998) *Crossing Bridges. Training resources for working with mentally ill parents and their children. Reader – for managers, practitioners and trainers.* p.72. Pavilion Publishing, Brighton.

1.18 The ability to differentiate the vulnerabilities and strengths of children at different ages and stages of development is critical in assessment. The neglect of some of these issues for adolescents is increasingly being remedied. Cleaver (2000a) provides summaries of research findings of the relevant factors for different age groups, including children over 10 (Table 2).

**Table 2[2]  Vulnerabilities and strengths for children aged 10–14 years and teenagers 15 years and over**

| Vulnerabilities | Strengths |
| --- | --- |
| Coping with puberty without support. | Factual information about puberty, sex and contraception. |
| Denying own needs and feelings. | A mutual friend. Unstigmatised support of relevant professionals. |
| An increased risk of psychological problems, behavioural disorders, suicidal behaviours and offending. Low self-esteem. | The ability to separate themselves either psychologically or physically from stressful situations. |
| Poor school attainment due to: difficulties in concentration, poor attendance in order to look after parents or younger children, unacceptable behaviour resulting in a pattern of school exclusion. | Regular school atttendance. Sympathetic, empathic and vigilant teachers. A champion who acts vigorously on behalf of the child. For those no longer in school, a job. |
| The fear that revealing family problems will lead to the family being broken up. This may result in increased isolation from friends and adults outside the family. | A mentor or trusted adult with whom the child can discuss sensitive issues. Practical and domestic help. |
| Increased risk of abuse. Inappropriate role models. | An alternative, safe and supportive residence for children and young people subjected to violence or the threat of violence. |

2.  Reproduced with kind permission of the author. From: Cleaver H (2000a) *When parents' issues influence their ability to respond to children's needs.* In Horwath J (ed) *The Child's World: Assessing Children in Need. The Reader.* The NSPCC, London.

## Children's perspectives

1.19 Finally, children's own perspectives on their experiences are an important source of knowledge. Increasingly, the validity of children's views on their lives is acknowledged in research. Children have views about what is happening to them. They attach meaning to events. They have wishes and feelings which must be taken into account and they will have ideas about the direction of decisions and the way in which those decisions are executed (for example, Butler and Williamson, 1994; Shaw, 1998;

Brandon et al, 1999; Department of Health, forthcoming). Thomas and Beckford (1999), in their study of adopted children speaking, emphasise the importance of work with children being 'underpinned by good adult-child and child-adult communication'. The responsibility for trying to establish effective communication lies firmly with the adults. They identify the following imperatives for the adults involved (pp.131–132):

- Express themselves simply and clearly and use concepts which are familiar to children;

- Match their explanations of new ideas to the children's age and levels of understanding;

- Be aware of the possible impact of emotional distress on children's understanding;

- Elicit children's fears and offer reassurances;

- Allow children plenty of opportunities for asking questions;

- Ask children for feedback to see if information and explanations have been remembered and understood;

- Repeat, simplify, expand and build on explanations if appropriate;

- Use communication tools such as games, prompt cards, books and videos.

Innovative materials for use with children and young peoples of different ages and in different circumstances have been developed which assist good communication. Examples are included in Chapter 4.

## Parental capacity

1.20    Optimal child development is dependent on the positive role of parents or caregivers from children' s birth to adulthood. However, it is recognised that there can be a diversity of family styles (Department of Health, 1989, p.7):

   Although some basic needs are universal, there can be a variety of ways of meeting them. Patterns of family life differ according to culture, class and community and these differences should be respected and accepted. There is no one perfect way to bring up children and care must be taken to avoid value judgements and stereo-typing.

1.21    Rosenfeld et al (1986) add a note of caution about understanding parents' behaviours. They emphasise that just because a behaviour is normative does not necessarily mean it is optimal for child development.

1.22    However, children's chances of achieving optimal outcomes will depend on their parents' capacities to respond appropriately to their needs at different stages of their lives. There are many factors in parents that may inhibit their responses to their children and prevent their providing parenting to a level necessary to promote optimal outcomes in children. The number of parents who set out to cause harm to their children is very small. The majority of parents, including most of those who neglect or maltreat their children, want to do the best for their children and have their best interests at heart. However, as Rutter (1974) (quoted by Utting (1995)) suggests:

Good parenting requires certain permitting circumstances. There must be the necessary life opportunities and facilities. Where these are lacking even the best parents may find it difficult to exercise these skills.

Most of the parents interviewed by Thoburn et al (2000) were well aware that their standard of parenting at times failed to meet their children's needs.

1.23 Belsky and Vondra (1989) identify the multiple determinants of parenting. They can be summarised as follows:

- **Individual**
  (parental personality, child characteristics)

- **Historical**
  (parental developmental history)

- **Social**
  (partner satisfaction, social support network)

- **Circumstantial**
  (poverty; job dissatisfaction; ignorance about child development)

1.24 There are, therefore, many factors that may inhibit parenting responses, including parents' life experiences as adults and in childhood. Reder and Duncan (1999) suggest that parents' own childhood experiences may spill over into adult life. For instance, experiences of rejection, abandonment, neglect and feeling unloved as a child may be associated with excessive reliance on others and fear of being left, or excessive distancing from others and fear of dependency in adulthood. As with children, it is important to understand both the nature of the adversity parents have experienced and the level of any protective factors which can build resilience in adult life to help overcome adversity. For example, the important research of Rutter and colleagues on intergenerational factors showed that the presence of a supportive partner in adulthood could help counteract negative experiences of growing up in care (Rutter and Rutter, 1992).

1.25 Some parents may have serious health problems or impairments which may place upon children responsibilities inappropriate to their years unless informal support and appropriate services are provided for the family, in consultation with the child (Aldridge and Becker, 1999; Tucker et al, 1999). It is therefore necessary for social workers to understand what may inhibit parental responses to children and what the consequences of that inappropriate response may be for children of different ages.

1.26 Research studies (Department of Health, 1995; Department of Health, forthcoming) have suggested that, among problems likely to affect parenting are mental illness, problem alcohol and drug use and domestic violence (Buchanan (ed), 1994; Cleaver and Freeman, 1995; Reder and Lucey, 1995; Falkov, 1996; Brandon et al, 1999; Cleaver et al, 1999; Thoburn et al, 2000; Department of Health, forthcoming). A study for the Department of Health by Falkov of local reviews of deaths and serious injuries to children revealed that in a significant proportion, mothers were suffering from identifiable mental illnesses (Falkov, 1996). Cleaver et al (1999) particularly emphasise the damaging effects for a child of living with and witnessing domestic violence between adult members of the household.

1.27   It is important, therefore, that practitioners understand the impact of parental responses on the particular child. A two year old may be at risk of significant harm from a parent whose practical caring skills are diminished by a misuse of drugs or alcohol but a sixteen year old in a similar situation may be able to remain relatively unharmed. Understanding the interaction between parents' responses and capabilities and children's needs is a key principle underpinning effective assessment and intervention. As Cleaver (2000a) points out, not all children are equally vulnerable to the adverse consequences of parental problems.

1.28   Research suggests (Cleaver et al, 1999) children are less likely to be adversely affected when parental problems are:

- Mild and of short duration;

- Not associated with family violence, conflict and disorganisation;

- Do not result in the family breaking up.

Children may also be protected when other responsible adults are involved in child care, or assume the role of the child's champion or mentor. Careful account should be taken, therefore, of the context within which the parent or parents may be experiencing problems and the impact of parental behaviour on the child.

1.29   Some parents may be directly responsible for maltreating their children. Bentovim (1998, p.57) argues that 'significant harm represents a major symptom of failure of adaptation by parents to their role':

It may be useful to think of significant harm generally as a compilation of significant events, both acute and long-standing, which interact with the child's ongoing development, and interrupt, alter, or impair physical and psychological development. Being the victim of significant harm is likely to have a profound effect on a child's view of themselves as a person, and on their future lives. Significant harm represents a major symptom of failure of adaptation by parents to their role, and also involves both the family and society.

1.30   Writers such as Adcock (1998) and Brandon et al (1999) draw an important distinction between significant harm and abuse. Adcock (1998, p.35) argues that:

Significant harm needs to be understood separately from child abuse or neglect, although the two may coexist. The two can be differentiated by the idea that child abuse describes *acts* and *omissions*, significant harm describes *effects*... Ill Treatment may lead to the impairment or likely impairment of health and development ... Some children may need protection to prevent the recurrence (of ill treatment); any child whose health or development has been impaired may need services to deal with consequences of this.

1.31   Not only parent figures or caregivers maltreat children. Additionally, children may be abused by siblings. Outside their families, children may also be at risk of encountering perpetrators. Utting (Department of Health and Welsh Office, 1997) has drawn attention to the particular dangers of child sexual abuse for children living away from home. It is important to understand why adults or other children maltreat children. Social workers should inform themselves about the characteristics of personality and behaviour, profiles and methods of perpetrators of different forms of child maltreatment, including physical, sexual and emotional abuse, both where children are living with their families and elsewhere (Department of Health, 2000a).

## Parents' Perspectives

1.32    Parents' views about their contact with child welfare and other statutory services have been well documented, particularly when there have been child protection concerns (for example, Cleaver and Freeman, 1995; Farmer and Owen, 1995; Jones and Ramchandani, 1999; Thoburn et al, 2000). Aldgate and Bradley (1999) in their study of short-term accommodation found how these experiences influenced parental worries about asking for help from social services when they needed assistance. Parents' worries were about:

- being vulnerable to child protection enquiries and being afraid of losing their children;

- being perceived as failed parents;

- the impact of using short term accommodation on their children and being detrimental to their future relationship with them.

1.33    The sense of losing control once child welfare agencies are involved is keenly felt by parents. They want help but not at the cost of forfeiting their parenting responsibilities. Ghate and Hazel (forthcoming) found in a national study of parenting in poor environments that parents' wish to stay in control of the delivery of support services was an overriding theme.

1.34    What parents value from child welfare agencies is clearly detailed in studies of family support services (see Butt and Box, 1998; McAuley, 1999; Social Services Inspectorate, 1999; Tunstill and Aldgate, 2000), in studies of contact (Cleaver, 2000b) and of court processes (Hunt et al 1999) and includes:

- communication which is open, honest, timely and informative;

- social work time with someone who listens, gives feedback, information, reassurance and advice, and is reliable;

- services which are practical, tailored to particular needs and accessible;

- an approach which re-inforces and does not undermine their parenting capacity.

These issues are explored further in later chapters in this practice guidance.

## Theories and myths of the individual in society

1.35    Alongside the theories concerned with the development of individuals are those related to the individual in society. There is a wealth of knowledge from sociological and psychological research which provides important background material for understanding the impact of negative factors such as social exclusion, racial and other discrimination, deviancy and unsafe communities on the children and families with whom practitioners will come in contact. Of particular relevance in assessment are sociological theories concerned with the issues of social exclusion and use or misuse of power, such as social constructionism and stereotyping. Writing on the identification of child abuse, for example, Parton (1987) discusses how the parameters of child abuse have changed over time.

1.36    Good outcomes for children have sometimes been blocked by assumptions which tend to stereotype families. This is especially pertinent in relation to black children. Ahmed et al (1986), for example, were among the first black British writers in social work to emphasise the negative impact of institutional racism on service provision for black children and their families. The picture from recent research is complex. Some research suggests that black and other minority ethnic groups are under-represented as service users receiving preventive and supportive social services (Tunstill and Aldgate, 2000). However, when black and minority ethnic families are referred to social services, it is less likely to be about concerns of maltreatment but more likely to be with a request for a specific service (Thoburn et al, 2000). The following chapter by Dutt and Phillips provides a helpful comparison of black and white families in relation to the assessment of children's needs. They draw attention to factors such as family structures, cultural values, and discuss the myths and realities of black family networks. Accurate information of this type helps to remove confusion and uncertainty and avoids stereotyping of children and families.

1.37    It is also important not to confuse theory with ideology. Work with children and families has sometimes been subject to fashionable ideologies which may dictate the style of work adopted. Ideological approaches, for example, 'all children should be in family based care because residential care is bad for them' or 'siblings should be kept together at all costs' should never get in the way of ethical and professional practice which discriminates effectively in relation to the developmental needs of a particular child.

## Wider family, community and environmental factors

1.38    The role of the wider family can be a significant source of support. Conversely, extended families may not always be supportive. Sometimes, even when families live nearby, links are not maintained (Aldgate and Bradley, 1999). Thoburn et al (2000) found that, at times, the stresses within the whole family were such that grandparents and other relatives could not find a way to help, or were too caught up in their own problems. Some parents do not always wish to acknowledge to their wider kin that they are not coping with a burgeoning problem. However, Brandon et al (1999) found that when problems became serious, extended family members are likely to rally round to provide protection and care.

1.39    Similarly, the contribution of the community in providing practical and emotional support to the immediate family also needs to be understood. Living in a supportive community may offer considerable help to parents. It may be important to chart both families' interrelationships over time and their current wider connections in the communities in which they live. Genograms and Ecomaps may be useful means of doing this with families (Appendices 2 and 3 respectively).

1.40    Social isolation, through an absence of both physical and emotional support, is an important factor in limiting adults' sense of wellbeing and control over their lives (see Argyle, 1992; Coohey, 1996; Aldgate and Bradley, 1999). Research from HomeStart has also suggested that social isolation is one of the major reasons for referral for befriending support (McAuley, 1999). A two year survey of referrals to HomeStart (Northern Ireland) indicated that the predominant referrers were health visitors and that the five main reasons for referrals were:

- Mother's mental health (with postnatal depression being most prevalent);
- Mother's physical health;
- Multiple births/multiple young children;
- Child/ren's special needs eg. health problems;
- Mother's isolation/loneliness.

1.41  Where social isolation is combined with fears for personal safety because of a hostile neighbourhood, cumulative negative factors can have an impact on parents' mental and physical health. Additionally, the part the wider family and others may play in organised abuse needs to be understood (Cleaver, 1996). This includes the threats to children from dangerous individuals in unsafe communities.

1.42  Finally, there is considerable evidence which catalogues the impact of the environment on parental capacity. The impact on families' health and wellbeing is well known (for example, Bradshaw, 1990; Utting, 1995; Acheson, 1998). The day to day meaning of living on a low income is summarised by Amin and Oppenheim (1992, p.36), who describe material disadvantage as:

> ...a kind of partial citizenship, since the effects of material deprivation make it very difficult to participate in society as a full member...

1.43  The importance of recognising the interface between families and the communities in which they live has recently been identified by the Social Exclusion Unit (1998, p.9):

> While most areas have benefited from rising living standards, the poorest neighbourhoods have tended to become more rundown, more prone to crime and more cut off from the labour market.

1.44  Writers such as Jack (1997) and Stevenson (1998) have been concerned at the omission of environmental considerations from the social work process. Research studies have shown the strong association between economic disadvantage and living conditions and the chances that children will fail to thrive (Utting, 1995; Iwaniec, 1996). Differences are clearly apparent in the health and educational development of children growing up in areas of deprivation. This has its impact both on young adults' ability to succeed as effective parents and directly on children themselves, through the standards of school available to them, the sub-culture of peer groups with whom they relate and the community facilities provided.

1.45  Holman at a conference in 1998 put it starkly: 'Poverty undermines parenting'. The meaning of living in continuing poverty is exemplified by Anita in her account of bringing up her children in an environment of social deprivation, in Holman's *Faith in the Poor* (1998, pp.96–98):

> Poverty is a terrible thing. I just cannot cope with what I am getting on income support. I just wish I could feed and clothe my children but it is impossible with what I receive . . . I am really worried about the kids growing up in Easterhouse . . . I know in my heart they will either turn to drugs or end up in prison. My kids keep asking to move. They are lovely kids and intelligent and I would dearly love to see

them make something of themselves . . . but what can I do with no money? My children don't stand a chance.

1.46 Bebbington and Miles (1989) have demonstrated how the cumulative effect of disadvantage can dramatically increase a child's chances of coming into the care system:

**Table 3  The cumulate effect of disadvantage**

| Child 'A' | Child 'B' |
| --- | --- |
| Aged 5–9 | Aged 5–9 |
| No dependence on social security benefits | Household head receives income support |
| Two parent family | Single adult household |
| Three or fewer children | Four or more children |
| White | Mixed ethnic origin |
| Owner occupied home | Privately rented home |
| More rooms than people | One or more persons per room |
| **Odds are 1 in 7,000** | **Odds are 1 in 10** |

1.47 The relationship between disability and disadvantage is also important and has not always been well understood. This is well evidenced in the study by Lawton (1998) of families with more than one disabled child (of which there are some 17,000 in the United Kingdom). Such families are:

- more likely to be single parents;
- less likely to be in work;
- more likely to be in semi-skilled or unskilled jobs;
- more likely to be dependent on income support;
- less likely to own their own home;
- more likely to report housing as unsuitable;
- more likely to have extra costs

This study serves to reinforce the importance of considering the wider context in which families are caring for and bringing up disabled children (issues which are discussed more fully in Chapter 3).

1.48 The evidence suggests that the families of many children in need who are most disadvantaged are those living in poverty, in poor housing, without adequate social supports and in the poorest, hostile neighbourhoods. These families face multiple stresses which are interlinked. McAuley (1999) includes the following example in her study.

> ### Example of interplay of factors causing stress
>
> The parents had two children under five years of age. The mother had had a medical condition for some time, but her health suddenly deteriorated, leaving her unable to walk. She had been admitted to hospital immediately. On her return home, she fell whilst attempting to walk in her home and broke her arm. Her husband had been off work with ill health. She went on to describe her predicament when the HomeStart Organiser first came to see her:
>
>> I was completely useless. I couldn't even, obviously with a plaster cast on, I couldn't do something as simple as wash myself. I could just about feed myself and no more. P (her husband) had to basically cut up my meals for me. I couldn't change S's nappies or wash or iron. Those were things I had always done and P was having to do that. And he couldn't do that and look after the kids. It just really . . . .everything sort of went to pot . . . It was every kind of stress and with him being off for two years with no wages, we couldn't pay someone to come in and help us . . . My kids have never been separated from me before . . When I came home (from hospital) they were extremely insecure . . they really took my hospitalisation majorly badly . . . Any kind of disappearance at all, be it only for a few seconds to the back garden, you know, the kids panicked and were in hysterics and had to be completely reassured.
>
> McAuley (1999, pp.33–34)

## Overarching theories and approaches that inform practice

1.49   Practitioners have the arduous task of making sense of the wealth of theory and knowledge informing their assessments. Psychodynamic and learning theories help to understand the inner and outer worlds of children and families, while eco-systems theory provides a very helpful framework to analyse the interconnections between personal and environmental factors which have an impact upon the lives of children and families. These are more fully discussed in Seden's review of the literature on assessment of children and their families (Department of Health, 2000b).

1.50   The ecological approach takes the view that individuals are connected to and interact with the environment in which they live. The approach is well established in the social sciences (Siporin, 1975; Maluccio, 1981; Garbarino, 1982). A key exponent of this theory, Bronfenbrenner (1979) outlines its relevance to social work with children and families. He places children's lives in the context of a series of systems: the immediate settings of home, school, friendship group and their interrelationship; local social structures which influence those settings; and the larger institutional patterns of economic, social, educational, legal and political systems. Updated applications of ecological theory are to be found in the paper by Jack (1997), in Stevenson's study of neglected children (1998), and in relation to child maltreatment by Jones and Ramchandani (1999).

1.51   Workers have at their disposal knowledge of human growth and development in children and families, knowledge of the environment and community and of the interaction between all these elements. A concrete example of how different and interconnecting knowledge and systems may be translated into practice in relation to child maltreatment comes from Jones and Ramchandani (1999) in Figure 3. Similarly helpful examples can be found in Crossing Bridges (Falkov (ed), 1998, p.75) and the work of Capaldi and Eddy (in press) in relation to children with conduct disorders.

1.52 As Cox (1993) and others have pointed out, what is significant for a family may be the processes generated by an event or events which may interact with the child's needs and the surrounding vulnerabilities and protective factors. The event or events may set off a cycle or chain of interaction. In assessing what is happening to a child and family, thought is required about the process which has been generated and the maintenance of momentum. The importance of **context** is therefore critical in understanding the relationship between outcomes and those events which act as stressors. Reder and Duncan (1999) provide a useful summary of the key issues which should be kept in mind during the assessment process:

---

**Key issues for assessment**

- Context gives meaning to behaviour

- Individuals exist in relationships to others

- Relationship and communication are a function of each other

- Current relationships arise out of historical influences

- Interactions revolve around the meaning of one person for another

- There is circularity between a person's inner and outer world

Reder and Duncan (1999)

---

1.53 Another way of understanding what is happening in family functioning draws from the systemic approach which has evolved from cybernetic theory or the study of communication. The theory focuses on people in their current social and economic context and the beliefs underpinning their behaviour. It seeks to explain human problems in terms of relationships rather than individual characteristics or pathology. Problems in systems often arise from attempts to adjust to life events and are linked to notions of circular and reciprocal cause and effect. The systemic practitioner, therefore, seeks to identify repetitive sequences of interaction which maintain and are maintained by the original or subsequent problems. Accounts of the development and use of the theory are found, for example, in Gorrell-Barnes (1994) and White and Epston (1990).

1.54 Both systems and ecological models consider how the support services, including social workers and other professionals, add to or detract from the family's coping mechanisms.

## Methods of intervention .

1.55 During the process of assessment, workers will be thinking about interventions that will best help children and families. The choice of intervention will be governed by many factors. Among these will be the appropriate application of social work methods. These methods have been developed from a range of psychosocial theories.

Figure 3  **A developmental and ecological perspective on child maltreatment**

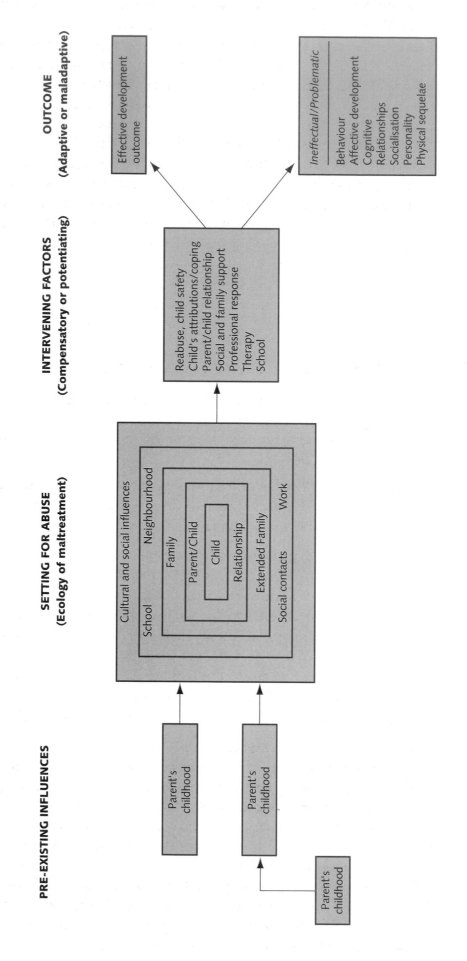

PRE-EXISTING INFLUENCES

SETTING FOR ABUSE
(Ecology of maltreatment)

INTERVENING FACTORS
(Compensatory or potentiating)

OUTCOME
(Adaptive or maladaptive)

Parent's childhood

Parent's childhood

Parent's childhood

Cultural and social influences
Neighbourhood
Family
School
Parent/Child
Child
Relationship
Extended Family
Work
Social contacts

Reabuse, child safety
Child's attributions/coping
Parent/child relationship
Social and family support
Professional response
Therapy
School

Effective development outcome

*Ineffectual/Problematic*
Behaviour
Affective development
Cognitive
Relationships
Socialisation
Personality
Physical sequelae

*Reproduced with kind permission of the authors.*
*From: Jones D and Ramchandani P (1999) Child Sexual Abuse. Informing Practice from Research. Radcliffe Medical Press, Abingdon.*

The methods include psychosocial casework, cognitive behavioural work, counselling, family therapy, task-centred casework, crisis intervention and so forth. Part of the assessment will be to think about which particular method will be best suited to the needs of individual children and their families. The approach must be eclectic. Workers may have their favoured approaches but it is not appropriate to use one method in all circumstances to the exclusion of all others. Choice of method should also be influenced by knowledge of what works in particular circumstances. For example, Jones and Ramchandani (1999), in writing about child sexual abuse, conclude that the 'best available evidence points to the use of focused therapies based on a cognitive-behavioural model being the most effective way of treating these symptoms'. However, they warn that 'no single therapy has demonstrable benefits for all children who have been sexually abused' (Jones and Ramchandani,1999, p.72). Texts based on clinical work like that of Jewett (1982) on helping children manage separation and loss, Fahlberg's (1991) work on children in transitions, and examples of clinical practice in direct work with children from Aldgate and Simmonds (1988) all have a major contribution to play in building up a repertoire of methods of intervention rooted in theory, research and good practice.

## Roles and tasks of child and family workers

1.56 Of course in practice it is very difficult to separate the boundaries between assessment and intervention. Having established what is happening to a child within the context of his or her family and environment and the impact on the child, the purpose of assessment will change (Jones, 1998, p.111):

> Later on, the process develops into an assessment of the likelihood of change, followed by whether such change is achieved. Looked at this way, assessment continues throughout intervention.

1.57 Another important dimension of assessing the appropriate intervention is the decision whether the child remains at home or is looked after away from home, and whether this should be on a short term or permanent basis. Where a child is looked after, it will be important to consider all the factors surrounding placement choice, including plans for reunification and adoption (Thoburn et al, 1986; Department of Health, 1989; Department of Health, 1991b; Department of Health, 1999). Any decisions which involve changes for children must take account of their developmental needs. Principles of stability and continuity are important for children at any level of intervention, as are principles of safeguarding and promoting children's welfare.

1.58 Furthermore, the communication skills and interactions required to gather information will inevitably trigger in some children and families the beginning of problem solving processes. Recent research on family support has suggested that a short encounter between a social worker and a family to assess difficulties may be in itself a problem solving experience. The exchange and synthesis of information between family members and the worker may be enough to help the family without further social work intervention. At the other end of the continuum, long-term help will be necessary for a significant number of families (Department of Health, forthcoming). Schofield and Brown (1999) and Thoburn et al (2000) urge that workers remember the importance of the professional relationship between worker and children and families in any direct encounter with families.

1.59 Methods of intervention are only part of the knowledge base that practitioners need for assessment. They are important because good assessments are built on an integration of theory and practice. Knowledge is being continually developed by research findings and the evolution of new and existing theories. These include knowledge about child development, parenting and the impact of parental difficulties, and the significance of environmental factors. Work with children and families does not take place within a vacuum but in an organisational and legislative context. Understanding the roles and tasks of a worker, not only within the context of his or her own agency but also taking account of the roles and tasks of other workers and the contexts of agencies which are likely to be contributing to the promotion of the welfare of the child, is another area of knowledge essential to the assessment process. In this respect, it is also important to take account of the impact of agency factors on outcomes for children.

1.60 Effective collaboration between workers in different agencies is notoriously difficult to achieve. Recognition that inter-agency co-operation is required is not new. Hallett and Stevenson (1980) cite 'a government circular (Home Office, 1950) on ill-treated children which recommended the establishment of children's co-ordinating committees' (p.1). However, the difficulties and 'failures' in inter-agency working have been well documented in reviews of individual cases of child maltreatment and in more broadly based research studies (Department of Health and Social Security, 1982; Department of Health, 1991a; Department of Health, 1995; Hallett, 1995). Hudson (2000) helpfully explores these issues, noting that governments have again and again exhorted public sector services to work more closely together (p.235):

> There is a paradox here, with 'collaboration' seen as both problem *and* solution – failure to work together is the problem, therefore the solution is to work together!

1.61 He gives a salutory reminder that the literature constantly focuses on the barriers to collaboration including structural, professional, financial, status and legitimacy factors, but that 'inter-organisational relationships are largely built upon *human* relationships' (p.254). Some of the important messages for collaborative working which practitioners should understand are summarised below:

**Collaborative Working: General Messages**

- Reciprocity is the basis of collaboration
- Collaboration is a continuum with choices
- Collaboration requires a consensus of stakeholders
- Collaboration requires an expression of purpose
- Trust is essential to collaborative success

Hudson et al (1999)

## The challenge of evidence based work

1.62 The Introduction to this practice guidance emphasised the importance placed on evidence based practice. This is a marked shift from thinking about evidence only as part of judicial processes. Rowe drew this out succinctly in *Patterns and Outcomes in Child Placement* (Department of Health, 1991b, pp.77–78):

> Social workers tend to think of evidence in terms of court hearings and reports, but evidence in the sense of 'facts which lead to conclusions' must be at the heart of every decision. The whole child care service, from strategic planning to monitoring of individual outcomes, is permeated by questions of evidence. Gathering, testing, recording and weighing evidence are tasks basic to professional competence, but are seldom addressed in these terms... Decisions can only be as good as the evidence on which they are based...

1.63 Throughout the *Framework for the Assessment of Children in Need and their Families* (Department of Health et al, 2000) and the materials produced to accompany the guidance, the sources of knowledge which have been used have been referenced and discussed to assist practitioners to develop their own knowledge base. However, evidence based practice also refers to the **process** whereby practitioners gather relevant information about what is happening to a child and use their knowledge from research findings, theoretical ideas and practical experience to arrive at a greater understanding of a particular child and family's experiences. Reder and Duncan (1999) provide a helpful discussion of this process, emphasising the importance of the application of knowledge at each stage of work with children and families. They refer to this as the development of a 'dialetic' mindset (p.98):

> Put at its simplest, assessment comes before action and the impact of actions needs to be monitored. Therefore, assessment should be an evolving process in which thought and action are reciprocal. Actions are guided by thought and the consequences of action are noted, considered and fed back to influence further action.

1.64 Thus, evidence based work also requires the careful use of knowledge gained **during** work with a child and family to undertake the task of determining what is most relevant in a family's situation, what is most significant for the child, the impact intervention is having and the judgement about when more or less action is required in the child's best interests.

1.65 Hunt et al (1999), in their study of the use of courts following the implementation of the Children Act 1989, explore the challenge of an evidence based approach for practitioners in that context (p.391):

> The new criteria for statutory intervention, for instance, and the emphasis on partnership with parents, place a premium on the capacity of social workers and their managers to evaluate evidence and manage risk, to develop skills at working with families in a voluntary framework and judging the point at which it is not viable. Once a case comes to court the social worker is expected to present coherent written evidence on what may well now be a more complex involvement with the family, be au fait with court procedures and be a competent witness even though the opportunities to accumulate court experiences are less frequent.

1.66 Although the principle of evidence based practice applies to all professionals who work with children and families, it is perhaps social work practitioners who are experiencing the challenge most keenly. It is essential for effective assessment of children in need and their families that social work is a confident profession, particularly in the context of inter-agency collaboration with other professionals. This requires social workers to be sure of their professional expertise and the knowledge on which they draw to form their professional judgements. Higham (Community Care, 1999) sums up this challenge:

> If social work is to develop further in the twenty-first century, practitioners must not rely soley on practice wisdom for decision making but use evidence based knowledge … Social work beyond the millennium needs to come of age. This will happen when social workers find an effective voice, develop new roles and establish a better knowledge base for their practice.

# APPENDIX 1

| MARY SHERIDAN | 1 MONTH | 3 MONTHS |
|---|---|---|
| **Posture and large movements** | Lies back with head to one side; arm and leg on same side outstretched, or both arms flexed; knees apart, soles of feet turned inwards.<br>Large jerky movements of limbs, arms more active than legs.<br>At rest, hands closed and thumb turned in.<br>Fingers and toes fan out during extenor movements of limbs.<br>When cheek touched, turns to same side; ear gently rubbed, turns head away.<br>When lifted or pulled to sit head falls loosely backwards.<br>Held sitting, head falls forward, with back in one complete curve.<br>Placed downwards on face, head immediately turns to side; arms and legs flexed under body, buttocks humped up.<br>Held standing on hard surface, presses down feet, straightens body and often makes reflex 'stepping' movements. | Now prefers to lie on back with head in mid-line. Limbs more pliable, movements smoother and more continuous.<br>Waves arms symmetrically. Hands now loosely open.<br>Brings hands together from side into mid-line over chest or chin.<br>Kicks vigorously, legs alternating or occasionally together. Held sitting, holds back straight, except in lumbar region, with head erect and steady for several seconds before bobbing forwards. Placed downwards on face lifts head and upper chest well up in mid-line, using forearms as support, and often scratching at table surface; legs straight, buttocks flat.<br>Held standing with feet on hard surface, sags at knees. |
| **Vision and fine movements** | Turns head and eyes towards light.<br>Stares expressionlessly at brightness of window or blank wall.<br>Follows pencil flash-lamp briefly with eyes at 1 foot.<br>Shuts eyes tightly when pencil light shone directly into them at 1–2 inches.<br>Notices silent dangling toy shaken in line of vision at 6–8 inches and follows its slow movement with eyes from side towards mid-line on level with face through approximately quarter circle, before head falls back to side.<br>Gazes at mother's nearby face when she feeds or talks to him with increasingly alert facial expression. | Visually very alert, particularly interested in nearby human faces.<br>Moves head deliberately to look around him.<br>Follows adult's movements near cot.<br>Follows dangling toy at 6–10 inches above face through half circle from side to side, and usually also vertically from chest to brow.<br>Watches movements of own hands before face and beginning to clasp and unclasp hands together in finger play.<br>Recognises feeding bottle and makes eager welcoming movements as it approaches his face.<br>Regards still objects within 6–10 inches for more than a second or two, but seldom fixates continuously.<br>Comerges eyes as dangling toy is moved towards face. Defensive blink shown. |
| **Hearing and speech** | Startled by sudden loud noises, stiffens, quivers, blinks, screws eyes up, extends limbs, fans out fingers and toes, and may cry.<br>Movements momentarily 'frozen', when small bell rung gently 3–5 inches from ear for 3–5 seconds, with 5 second pauses; may 'corner' eyes towards sound.<br>Stops whimpering to sound of nearby soothing human voice, but not when screaming or feeding.<br>Cries lustily when hungry or uncomfortable.<br>Utters little gutteral noises when content.<br>(*Note:* Deaf babies also cry and vocalise in this reflex way, but if very deaf do not usually show startle reflex to sudden noises. Blind babies may also move eyes towards a sound-making toy. Vision should always be checked separately.) | Sudden loud noises still distress, provoking blinking, screwing up of eyes, crying and turning away.<br>Definite quietening or smiling to sound of mother's voice before she touches him, but not when screaming.<br>Vocalises freely when spoken to or pleased.<br>Cries when uncomfortable or annoyed.<br>Quietens to tinkle of spoon in cup or to bell rung gently out of sight for 3–5 seconds at 6–12 inches from ear.<br>May turn eyes and head towards sound; brows may wrinkle and eyes dilate.<br>Often licks lips in response to sounds of preparation for feeding.<br>Shows excitement at sound of approaching footsteps, running bath water, voices, etc.,<br>(*Note:* Deaf baby, instead, may be obviously startled by mother's sudden appearance beside cot.) |
| **Social behaviour and play** | Sucks well.<br>Sleeps much of the time when not being fed or handled.<br>Expression still vague, but becoming more alert, progressing to social smiling about 5–6 weeks.<br>Hands normally closed, but if opened, grasps examiner's finger when palm is touched.<br>Stops crying when picked up and spoken to.<br>Mother supports head when carrying, dressing and bathing. | Fixes eyes unblinkingly on mother's face when feeding.<br>Beginning to react to familiar situations – showing by smiles, coos, and excited movements that he recognises preparation for feeds, baths, etc.<br>Responds with obvious pleasure to friendly handling, especially when accompanied by playful tickling and vocal sounds.<br>Holds rattle for few moments when placed in hand, but seldom capable of regarding it at same time.<br>Mother supports at shoulders when dressing and bathing. |

23

# Chart illustrating the developmental progress of infants and young children – continued

| | 6 MONTHS | 9 MONTHS |
|---|---|---|
| **Posture and large movements** | Lying on back, raises head from pillow.<br>Lifts legs into vertical and grasps foot.<br>Sits with support in cot or pram and turns head from side to look around him.<br>Moves arms in brisk and purposeful fashion and holds them up to be lifted.<br>When hands grasped braces shoulders and pulls himself up.<br>Kicks strongly, legs alternating.<br>Can roll over, front to back.<br>Held sitting, head is firmly erect, and back straight.<br>May sit alone momentarily.<br>Placed downwards on face lifts head and chest well up, supporting himself on extended arms.<br>Held standing with feet touching hard surface bears weight on feet and bounces up and down actively. | Sits alone for 10–15 minutes on floor.<br>Can turn body to look sideways while stretching out to grasp dangling toy or to pick up toy from floor.<br>Arms and legs very active in cot, pram and bath.<br>Progresses on floor by rolling or squirming.<br>Attempts to crawl on all fours.<br>Pulls self to stand with support.<br>Can stand holding on to support for a few moments, but cannot lower himself.<br>Held standing, steps purposefully on alternate feet. |
| **Vision and fine movements** | Visually insatiable: moves head and eyes eagerly in every direction.<br>Eyes move in unison: squint now abnormal.<br>Follows adult's movements across room.<br>Immediately fixates interesting small objects within 6–12 inches (eg, toy, bell, wooden cube, spoon, sweet) and stretches out both hands to grasp them.<br>Uses whole hand in palmar grasp.<br>When toys fall from hand over edge of cot forgets them.<br>(Watches rolling balls of 2 to 1/4 inch diameter at 10 feet). | Very observant.<br>Stretches out, one hand leading, to grasp small objects immediately on catching sight of them.<br>Manipulates objects with lively interest, passing from hand to hand, turning over, etc.<br>Pokes at small sweet with index finger. Grasps sweets, string, etc., between finger and thumb in scissor fashion.<br>Can release toy by pressing against firm surface, but cannot yet put down precisely.<br>Searches in correct place for toys dropped within reach of hands.<br>Looks after toys falling over edge of pram or table.<br>Watches activities of adults, children and animals within 10–12 feet with eager interest for several seconds at a time.<br>(Watches rolling balls 2 1/8 inches at 10 feet.) |
| **Hearing and speech** | Turns immediately to mother's voice across room.<br>Vocalises tunefully and often, using single and double syllables, eg. ka, muh, goo, der, adah, er-lah.<br>Laughs, chuckles and squeals aloud in play<br>Screams with annoyance.<br>Shows evidence of response to different emotional tones of mother's voice.<br>Responds to baby hearing test at 1 1/2 feet from each ear by correct visual localisation, but may show slightly brisker response on one side.<br>(Tests employed – voice, rattle, cup and spoons, paper, bell; 2 seconds with 2 seconds pause.) | Vocalises deliberately as means of interpersonal communication.<br>Shouts to attract attention, listens, then shouts again.<br>Babbles tunefully, repeating syllables in long strings (mam-man, bab-bab, dad-dad, etc.)<br>Understands 'No-No' and 'Bye-Bye'.<br>Tries to imitate adults' playful vocal sounds, eg. smacking lips, cough, brr, etc.<br>(Immediate localising response to baby hearing tests at 3 feet from ear and above and below ear level.) |
| **Social behaviour and play** | Hands competent to reach for and grasp small toys.<br>Most often uses a two-handed, scooping-in approach, but occasionally a single hand.<br>Takes everything to mouth.<br>Beginning to find feet interesting and even useful in grasping.<br>Puts hands to bottle and pats it when feeding.<br>Shakes rattle deliberately to make it sound, often regarding it closely at same time.<br>Still friendly with strangers but occasionally shows some shyness or even slight anxiety, especially if mother is out of sight. | Holds, bites and chews biscuits.<br>Puts hands round bottle or cup when feeding.<br>Tries to grasp spoon when being fed.<br>Throws body back and stiffens in annoyance or resistance.<br>Clearly distinguishes strangers from familiars, and requires reassurance before accepting their advances.<br>Clings to known adult and hides face.<br>Still takes everything to mouth.<br>Seizes bell in one hand, imitates ringing action, waving or banging it on table, pokes clapper or 'drinks' from bowl.<br>Plays peek-a-boo.<br>Holds out toy held in hand to adult, but cannot yet give.<br>Finds partially hidden toy.<br>May find toy hidden under cup.<br>Mother supports at lower spine when dressing. |

| | 12 MONTHS | 15 MONTHS |
|---|---|---|
| **Posture and large movements** | Sits well and for indefinite time.<br>Can rise to sitting position from lying down.<br>Crawls rapidly, usually on all fours.<br>Pulls to standing and lets himself down again holding on to furniture.<br>Walks round furniture stepping sideways.<br>Walks with one or both hands held.<br>May stand alone for a few moments.<br>May walk alone. | Walks unevenly with feet wide apart, arms slightly flexed and held above head or at shoulder level to balance.<br>Starts alone, but frequently stopped by falling or bumping into furniture.<br>Lets himself down from standing to sitting by collapsing backwards with bump, or occasionally by falling forward on hands and then back to sitting.<br>Can get to feet alone.<br>Crawls upstairs.<br>Kneels unaided or with slight support on floor and in pram, cot and bath.<br>May be able to stoop to pick up toys from floor. |
| **Vision and fine movements** | Picks up small objects, eg blocks, string, sweets and crumbs, with precise pincer grasp of thumb and index finger.<br>Throws toys deliberately and watches them fall to ground.<br>Looks in correct place for toys which roll out of sight.<br>Points with index finger at objects he wants to handle or which interest him.<br>Watches small toy pulled along floor across room 10 feet away.<br>Out of doors watches movements of people, animals, motor cars, etc., with prolonged intent regard.<br>Recognises familiars approaching from 20 feet or more away.<br>Uses both hands freely, but may show preference for one.<br>Clicks two bricks together in imitation.<br>(Watches rolling balls $2^{1}/_{8}$ inches at 10 feet.) | Picks up string, small sweets and crumbs neatly between thumb and finger.<br>Builds tower of two cubes after demonstration.<br>Grasps crayon and imitates scribble after demonstration.<br>Looks with interest at pictures in book and pats page.<br>Follows with eyes path of cube or small toy swept vigorously from table.<br>Watches small toy pulled across floor up to 12 feet.<br>Points imperiously to objects he wishes to be given.<br>Stands at window and watches events outside intently for several minutes.<br>(Watches and retrieves rolling balls of $2^{1}/_{8}$ inches at 10 feet.) |
| **Hearing and speech** | Knows and immediately turns to own name.<br>Babbles loudly, tunefully and incessantly.<br>Shows by suitable movements and behaviour that he understands several words in usual context (eg. own and family names, walk, dinner, pussy, cup, spoon, ball, car).<br>Comprehends simple commands associated with gesture (give it to daddy, come to mummy, say bye-bye, clap hands, etc.)<br>Imitates adult's playful vocalisations with gleeful enthusiasm.<br>May hand examine common objects on request, eg. spoon, cup, ball, shoe.<br>(Immediate response to baby tests at 3–$4^{1}/_{2}$ feet but rapidly habituates.) | Jabbers loudly and freely, using wide range of inflections and phonetic units.<br>Speaks 2–6 recognisable words and understands many more.<br>Vocalises wishes and needs at table.<br>Points to familiar persons, animals, toys, etc., when requested.<br>Understands and obeys simple commands (eg. shut the door, give me the ball, get your shoes).<br>(Baby test $4^{1}/_{2}$–6 feet.) |
| **Social behaviour and play** | Drinks from cup with little assistance. Chews.<br>Holds spoon but usually cannot use it alone.<br>Helps with dressing by holding out arm for sleeve and foot for shoe.<br>Takes objects to mouth less often.<br>Puts wooden cubes in and out of cup or box.<br>Rattles spoon in cup in imitation.<br>Seizes bell by handle and rings briskly in imitation, etc.<br>Listens with obvious pleasure to percussion sounds.<br>Repeats activities to reproduce effects.<br>Gives toys to adult on request and sometimes spontaneously. Finds hidden toy quickly.<br>Likes to be constantly within sight and hearing of adult.<br>Demonstrates affection to familiars.<br>Waves 'bye-bye' and claps hands in imitation or spontaneously.<br>Child sits, or sometimes stands without support, while mother dresses. | Holds cup when adult gives and takes back.<br>Holds spoon, brings it to mouth and licks it, but cannot prevent its turning over. Chews well.<br>Helps more constructively with dressing.<br>Indicates when he has wet pants.<br>Pushes large wheeled toy with handle on level ground.<br>Seldom takes toy to mouth.<br>Repeatedly casts objects to floor in play or rejection, usually without watching fall.<br>Physically restless and intensely curious.<br>Handles everything within reach.<br>Emotionally labile.<br>Closely dependent upon adult's reassuring presence.<br>Needs constant supervision to protect child from dangers of extended exploration and exploitation of environment. |

| | 18 MONTHS | 2 YEARS |
|---|---|---|
| **Posture and large movements** | Walks well with feet only slightly apart, starts and stops safely. Runs stifly upright, eyes fixed on ground 1–2 yards ahead, but cannot continue to run round obstacles. Pushes and pulls large toys, boxes, etc., round floor. Can carry large doll or teddy-bear while walking and sometimes two. Backs into small chair or slides in sideways. Climbs forward into adult's chair then turns round and sits. Walks upstairs with helping hand. Creeps backwards down stairs. Occasionally bumps down a few steps on buttocks facing forwards. Picks up toy from floor without falling. | Runs safely on whole foot, stopping and starting with ease and avoiding obstacles. Squats to rest or to play with object on ground and rises to feet without using hands. Walks backwards pulling large toy. Pulls wheeled toy by cord. Climbs on furniture to look out of window or open doors, etc., and can get down again. Walks upstairs and down holding on to rail and wall; two feet to a step. Throws small ball without falling. Walks into large ball when trying to kick it. Sits astride large wheeled toy and propels forward with feet on ground. |
| **Vision and fine movements** | Picks up small sweets, beads, pins, threads, etc., immediately on sight, with delicate pincer grasp. Spontaneous scribble when given crayon and paper, using preferred hand. Builds tower of three cubes after demonstration. Enjoys simple picture book, often recognising and putting finger on coloured items on page. Turns pages 2 or 3 at a time. Fixes eyes on a small dangling toy up to 10 feet. (May tolerate this test with each eye separately.) Points to distant interesting objects out of doors. (Watches and retrieves rolling balls 2–1/2 inches at 10 feet.) (Possibly recognises special miniature toys at 10 feet.) | Picks up pins and thread, etc., neatly and quickly. Removes paper wrapping from small sweet. Builds lower of six cubes (or 6+). Spontaneous circular scribble and dots when given paper and pencil. Imitates vertical line (and sometimes V). Enjoys picture books, recognising fine details in favourite pictures. Turns pages singly. Recognises familiar adults in photograph after once shown. Hand preference becoming evident. (Immediately catches sight of, and names special miniature toys at 10 feet distance. Will now usually tolerate this test with each eye separately.) (Watches and retrieves rolling balls 2 – $1/8$ inches at 10 feet.) |
| **Hearing and speech** | Continues to jabber tunefully to himself at play. Uses 6–20 recognisable words and understands many more. Echoes prominent or last word addressed to him. Demands desired objects by pointing accompanied by loud, urgent vocalisation or single words. Enjoys nursery rhymes and tries to join in. Attempts to sing. Shows his own or doll's hair, shoe, nose (Possibly special 5 toy test. Possibly 4 animals picture test.) | Uses 50 or more recognisable words and understands many more. Puts 2 or more words together to form simple sentences. Refers to himself by name. Talks to himself continually as he plays. Echo(s) a almost constant, with one or more stressed words repeated. Constantly asking names of objects. Joins in nursery rhymes and songs. Shows correctly and repeats words for hair, hand, feet, nose, eyes, mouth, shoe on request. (6 toy test, 4 animals picture test.) |
| **Social behaviour and play** | Lifts and holds cup between both hands. Drinks without spilling. Hands cup back to adult. Choose well. Holds spoon and gets food to mouth. Takes off shoes, socks, hat. Indicates toilet needs by restlessness and vocalisation. Bowel control usually attained. Explores environment energetically. No longer takes toys to mouth. Remembers where objects belong. Casts objects to floor in play or anger less often. Briefly imitates simple activities, e.g. reading book, kissing doll, brushing floor. Plays contentedly alone, but likes to be near adult. Emotionally still very dependent upon familiar adult, especially mother. Alternates between clinging and resistance. | Lifts and drinks from cup and replaces on table. Spoon-feeds without spilling. Asks for food and drink. Chews competently. Puts on hat and shoes. Verbalises toilet needs in reasonable time. Dry during day. Turns door handles. Often runs outside to explore. Follows mother round house and copies domestic activities in simultaneous play. Engages in simple make-believe activities. Constantly demanding mother's attention. Clings lightly in affection, fatigue or fear. Tantrums when frustrated but attention readily distracted. Defends own possessions with determination. As yet no idea of sharing. Plays near other children but not with them. Resentful of attention shown to other children. |

| | 2¹/₂ YEARS | 3 YEARS |
|---|---|---|
| **Posture and large movements** | Walks upstairs alone but downstairs holding rail, two feet to a step.<br>Runs well straight forward and climbs easy nursery apparatus.<br>Pushes and pulls large toys skillfully, but has difficulty in steering them round obstacles.<br>Jumps with two feet together.<br>Can stand on tiptoe if shown.<br>Kicks large ball.<br>Sits on tricycle and steers with hands, but still usually propels with feet on ground. | Walks alone upstairs with alternating feet and downstairs with two feet to step.<br>Usually jumps from bottom step.<br>Climbs nursery apparatus with agility.<br>Can turn round obstacles and corners while running and also while pushing and pulling large toys.<br>Rides tricycle and can turn wide corners on it.<br>Can walk on tiptoe.<br>Stands momentarily on one foot when shown.<br>Sits with feet crossed at ankles. |
| **Vision and fine movements** | Picks up pins, threads, etc., with each eye covered separately.<br>Builds tower of seven (or 7+) cubes and lines blocks to form 'train'.<br>Recognises minute details in picture books.<br>Imitates horizontal line and circle (also usually T and V).<br>Paints strokes, dots and circular shapes on easel.<br>Recognises himself in photographs when once shown.<br>Recognises miniature toys and retrieves balls 2¹/₈ inches at 10 feet, each eye separately.<br>(May also match special single letter-cards V, O, T, H at 10 feet.) | Picks up pins, threads, etc., with each eye covered separately.<br>Builds tower of nine cubes, also (3¹/₂) bridge of three from model.<br>Can close fist and wiggle thumb in imitation. R and L.<br>Copies circle (also V, H, T). Imitates cross.<br>Draws man with head and usually indication of features or one other part.<br>Matches two or three primary colours (usually red and yellow correct, but may confuse blue and green).<br>Paints 'pictures' with large brush on easel.<br>Cuts with scissors.<br>(Recognises special miniature toys at 10 feet. Performs single-letter vision test at 10 feet. Five letters.) |
| **Hearing and speech** | Uses 200 or more recognisable words but speech shows numerous infantilisms.<br>Knows full name.<br>Talks intelligibly to himself at play concerning events happening here and now.<br>Echolalia persists.<br>Continually asking questions beginning 'What?', 'Where?'.<br>Uses pronouns, I, me and you.<br>Stuttering in eagerness common.<br>Says a few nursery rhymes.<br>Enjoys simple familiar stories read from picture book.<br>(6 toy test, 4 animal picture test, 1st cube test. Full doll vocabulary.) | Large intelligible vocabulary but speech still shows many infantile phonetic substitutions. Gives full name and sex, and (sometimes) age.<br>Uses plurals and pronouns.<br>Still talks to himself in long monologues mostly concerned with the immediate present, including make-believe activities.<br>Carries on simple conversations, and verbalises past experiences.<br>Asks many questions beginning 'What?', 'Where?', 'Who?'.<br>Listens eagerly to stories and demands favourites over and over again.<br>Knows several nursery rhymes.<br>(7 toy test, 4 animals picture test. 1st or 2nd cube test, 6 'high frequency' word pictures.) |
| **Social behaviour and play** | Eats skilfully with spoon and may use fork.<br>Pulls down pants or knickers at toilet, but seldom able to replace.<br>Dry through night if lifted.<br>Very active, restless and rebellious.<br>Throws violent tantrums and when thwarted or unable to express urgent need and less easily distracted.<br>Emotionally still very dependent upon adults.<br>Prolonged domestic make-believe play (putting dolls to bed, washing clothes, driving motor cars, etc.) but with frequent reference to friendly adult.<br>Watches other children at play interestedly and occasionally joins in for a few minutes, but little notion of sharing playthings or adult's attention. | Eats with fork and spoon.<br>Washes hands, but needs supervision in drying.<br>Can pull pants and knickers down and up, but needs help with buttons.<br>Dry through night.<br>General behaviour more amenable.<br>Affectionate and confiding.<br>Likes to help with adult's activities in house and garden.<br>Makes effort to keep his surroundings tidy.<br>Vividly realised make-believe play including invented people and objects.<br>Enjoys floor play with bricks, boxes, toy trains and cars, alone or with siblings.<br>Joins in play with other children in and outdoors.<br>Understands sharing playthings, sweets, etc.<br>Shows affection for younger siblings.<br>Shows some appreciation of past and present. |

| | 4 YEARS | 5 YEARS |
|---|---|---|
| **Posture and large movements** | Turns sharp corners running, pushing and pulling. Walks alone up and downstairs, one foot per step. Climbs ladders and trees. Can run on tiptoe. Expert rider of tricycle. Hops on one foot. Stands on one foot 3–5 seconds. Arranges or picks up objects from floor by bending from waist with knees extended. | Runs lightly on toes. Active and skilful in climbing, sliding, swinging, digging and various 'stunts'. Skips on alternative feet. Dances to music. Can stand on one foot 8–10 seconds. Can hop 2–3 yards forwards on each foot separately. Grips strongly with either hand. |
| **Vision and fine movements** | Picks up pins, thread, crumbs, etc., with each eye covered separately. Builds tower of 10 or more cubes and several 'bridges' of three on request. Builds three steps with six cubes after demonstration. Imitates spreading of hand and bringing thumb into opposition with each finger in turn, R and L. Copies cross (also V, H, T and O). Draws man with head, legs, features, trunk and (often) arms. Draws very simple house. Matches and names four primary colours correctly. (Single-letter vision test at 10 feet, seven letters: also near chart to bottom). | Picks up minute objects when each eye is covered separately. Builds three steps with six cubes from model. Copies square and triangle (also letters; V, T, H, O, X, L, A, C, U, Y). Writes a few letters spontaneously. Draws recognisable man with head, trunk, legs, arms and features. Draws simple house with door, windows, roof and chimney. Counts fingers on one hand with index finger of other. Names four primary colours and matches 10 or 12 colours. (Full nine-letter vision chart at 20 feet and near test to bottom.) |
| **Hearing and speech** | Speech completely intelligible. Shows only a few infantile substitutions usually k/t/th/f/s and r/l/w/y groups). Gives connected account of recent events and experiences. Gives name, sex, home address and (usually) age. Eternally asking questions 'Why?' 'When?', 'How?' and meanings of words. Listens to and tells long stories sometimes confusing fact and fantasy. (7 toy test, 1st picture vocabulary test, 2nd cube test. 6 'high frequency' word pictures.) | Speech fluent and grammatical. Articulation correct except for residual confusions of s/f/th and r/l/w/y groups. Loves stories and acts them out in detail later. Gives full name, age and home address. Gives age and (usually) birthday. Defines concrete nouns by use. Asks meaning of abstract words. (12 'high frequency' picture vocabulary or word lists. 3rd cube test, 6 sentences.) |
| **Social behaviour and play** | Eats skilfully with spoon and fork. Washes and dries hands. Brushes teeth. Can undress and dress except for back buttons, laces and ties. General behaviour markedly self-willed. Inclined to verbal impertinence when wishes crossed but can be affectionate and compliant. Strongly dramatic play and dressing-up favoured. Constructive out-of-doors building with any large material to hand. Needs other children to play with and is alternately co-operative and aggressive with them as with adults. Understands taking turns. Shows concern for younger siblings and sympathy for playmates in distress. Appreciates past, present and future. | Uses knife and fork. Washes and dries face and hands, but needs help and supervision for rest. Undresses and dresses alone. General behaviour more sensible, controlled and responsibly independent. Domestic and dramatic play continued from day to day. Plans and builds constructively. Floor games very complicated. Chooses own friends. Co-operative with companions and understands need for rules and fair play. Appreciates meaning of clock time in relation to daily programme. Tender and protective towards younger children and pets. Comforts playmates in distress. |

Reprinted from *Reports on Public Health and Medical Subjects* No 102.
HMSO 1960, revised 1975. In Department of Health (1988) Protecting Children.
A Guide for Social Workers undertaking a Comprehensive Assessment, pp.88–93.
HMSO, London.

# APPENDIX 2 Genogram

## Genogram symbols

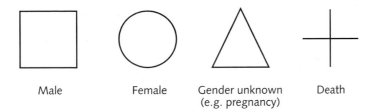

Male      Female      Gender unknown (e.g. pregnancy)      Death

## Genogram symbols

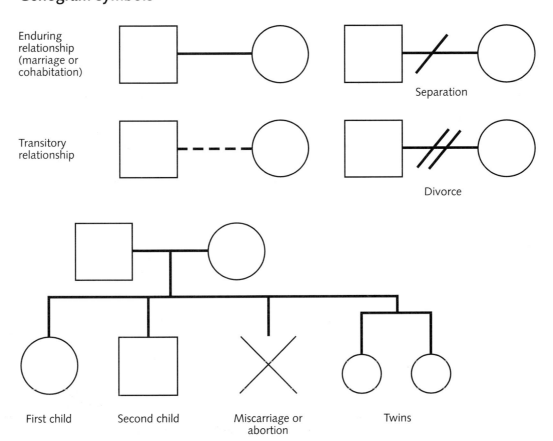

Enduring relationship (marriage or cohabitation)

Separation

Transitory relationship

Divorce

First child      Second child      Miscarriage or abortion      Twins

A dotted line should be drawn around the people who currently live in the same house.

### Compiling a genogram

A genogram of family tree covering three or more generations may be compiled using these symbols. Other relatives in addition to parents and children can be involved in compiling the genogram. More than one session may be needed if the exercise is used to discuss the family's history in detail and to enter significant dates and other information. Working on a genogram also provides the practitioner with an opportunity to observe family relationships, for example how open family members are with each other, how well they respond to each other's needs, how flexible they are and how much they know about each other.

# APPENDIX 3  Ecomap

■  Place child or couple or family in central circle.

■  Identify important people or organisations and draw circles as needed

■  Draw lines between circles where connections exist

■  Use different types of lines to indicate the nature of the link or relationship

——— = strong

- - - - = weak

••••• = stressful

# References – Chapter 1

Acheson D (1998) *Independent Inquiry into Inequalities in Health.* The Stationery Office, London.

Adcock M (1998) *Significant harm: implications for local authorities.* In Adcock M and White R (eds) (1998) *Significant Harm: its management and outcome.* pp.33–56. Significant Publications, Croydon.

Ahmed S, Cheetham J and Small J (ed) (1986) *Social Work with Black Children and their Families.* Batsford Ltd, London.

Aldgate J and Bradley M (1999) *Supporting Families through Short Term Fostering.* The Stationery Office, London.

Aldgate J and Simmonds J (eds) (1988) *Direct Work with Children: a Guide for Social Work Practitioners.* Batsford, London.

Aldridge J and Becker S (1999) Children as carers: the impact of parental illness on children's caring roles. *Journal of Family Therapy.* **21**: 303–320.

Amin K and Oppenheim C (1992) *Poverty in Black and White: Deprivation in Ethnic Minorities.* Child Poverty Action Group, London.

Argyle M (1992) *The Social Psychology of Everyday Life.* Routledge, London.

British Agencies for Adoption and Fostering (1999) *Making Good Assessments. Preparing for Permanence – A Practical Resource Guide.* BAAF, London.

Bandura A (1997) *Social Learning Theory.* Prentice-Hall, Englewood, NJ.

Bebbington A and Miles J (1989) The Background of Children who enter Local Authority Care. *British Journal of Social Work* **19**: 5, pp.349–368.

Belsky Y J and Vondra J (1989) *Lessons from child abuse: The determinants of parenting.* In Cicchetti D and Carlson V (eds) (1989) *Child Maltreatment: Theory and Research on the Causes and Consequences of Child Abuse and Neglect.* Cambridge University Press, New York.

Bentovim A (1998) *Significant Harm in Context.* In Adcock M and White R (eds) (1998) *Significant Harm: its Management and Outcome.* pp.57–89. Significant Publications, Croydon.

Bowlby J (1969) *Attachment and Loss, Vol I Attachment.* Hogarth Press, London

Bowlby J (1973) *Attachment and Loss, Vol II Separation: Anxiety and Anger.* Basic Books, New York.

Bowlby J (1980) *Attachment and Loss, Vol III Loss: Sadness and Depressions.* Basic Books, New York.

Bradshaw J (1990) *Child Poverty and Deprivation in the UK.* NCB, London.

Brandon M, Lewis A, Thoburn J and Way A (1999) *Safeguarding Children with the Children Act 1989.* The Stationery Office, London.

Brearley J (1991) *Counselling and Social Work.* Open University Press, Buckingham.

Bronfonbrenner U (1979) *The Ecology of Human Development: Experiments by Nature and Design.* Harvard University Press, Cambridge.

Buchanan A (1999) *What works for Troubled Children. Family support for children with emotional and behavioural problems.* Barnardo's, London.

Buchanan A (ed) (1994) *Partnership in Practice.* Avebury, Aldershot.

Buchanan A and Hudson B L (1998) *Parenting, Schooling and Children's Behaviour – interdisciplinary approaches.* Ashgate, Hampshire.

Butler I and Williamson H (1994) *Children Speak: children, trauma and social work.* Longman, Essex. In NSPCC in association with Chailey Heritage and Department of Health (1997) *Turning Points: A Resource Pack for Communicating with Children. Introduction.* pp.1–2. The NSPCC, London.

Butt J and Box C (1998) *Family Centred. A study of the use of family centres by black families.* REU, London.

Capaldi D and Eddy M (in press) *Improving Children's Long Term Well-being by Preventing Anti-Social Behaviour.* In Buchannan A and Hudson B L (in press) *Promoting the Emotional Well-being of Children. Messages from Research.* Oxford University Press, Oxford.

Carlson V, Cicchetti D, Barnett D and Braunwald K (1989) Disorganised/ Disoriented attachment relationships in maltreatment infants. *Developmental Psychology.* **25**: 525–531.

Cleaver H (1991) *Vunerable Children in Schools.* Dartmouth, Aldershot.

Cleaver H (1996) *Child Abuse which involved wider kin and family friends.* In Bibby P (ed) *Organised Abuse: The Current Debate.* Ashgate, Aldershot.

Cleaver H (2000a) *When parents' issues influence their ability to respond to children's needs.* In Horwath J (ed) *The Child's World: Assessing Children in Need. The Reader.* The NSPCC, London.

Cleaver H (2000b) *Fostering Family Contact: a study of children, parents and foster carers.* The Stationery Office, London.

Cleaver H and Freeman P (1995) *Parental Perspectives in Cases of Suspected Child Abuse.* HMSO, London.

Cleaver H, Unell I and Aldgate J (1999) *Children's Needs – Parenting Capacity: The impact of parental mental illness, problem alcohol and drug use, and domestic violence on children's development.* The Stationery Office, London.

Coohey C (1996) Child Maltreatment: Testing the social isolation hypothesis. *Child Abuse and Neglect.* **20**: 241–254.

Cox A (1993) Preventive aspects of child psychiatry. *Archives of Disease in Childhood.* **63**: 691–701.

Crittenden P M and Ainsworth M D S (1989) *Child Maltreatment and Attachment.* In Cicchetti D and Carlson V (eds) *Handbook of Child Maltreatment: Clinical and Theorectical Perspectives.* pp.432–463. Cambridge, New York.

Department of Health (1989) *The Care of Children: Principles and Practice in Regulations and Guidance.* HMSO, London.

Department of Health (1991a) *Child Abuse. A Study of Inquiry Reports 1980–1989.* HMSO, London.

Department of Health (1991b) *Patterns and Outcomes in Child Placement. Messages from current research and their implications.* HMSO, London.

Department of Health (1995) *Child Protection: Messages from Research.* HMSO, London.

Department of Health (1996) *Focus on Teenagers: Research into Practice.* HMSO, London.

Department of Health (1999) *Adoption Now: Messages from Inspection.* Wiley, Chichester.

Department of Health (2000a) *towards safer care. Training and Resource Pack.* The Department of Health, London.

Department of Health (2000b) *Studies which inform the development of the Framework for the Assessment of Children in Need and their Families.* The Stationery Office, London.

Department of Health (forthcoming) *The Children Act 1989 Now: Messages from Research.* The Stationery Office, London.

Department of Health, the Department of Education and Employment and the Home Office (2000) *Framework for the Assessment of Children in Need and their Families.* The Stationery Office, London.

Department of Health and Social Security (1982) *Child Abuse: A Study of Inquiry Reports.* HMSO, London.

Department of Health and the Welsh Office (1997) *People Like Us. Report of the Review of the Safeguards for Children Living Away from Home.* The Stationery Office, London.

Fahlberg V I (1981) *Attachment and Separation.* BAAF, London.

Fahlberg V I (1991) *A Child's Journey through Placement.* BAAF, London

Falkov A (1996) *A Study of Working Together "Part 8" Reports: Fatal child abuse and parental psychiatric disorder.* Department of Health – ACPC Series I. Department of Health, London.

Falkov A (ed) (1998) *Crossing Bridges – Training resources for working with mentally ill parents and their children. Reader – for managers, practitioners and trainers.* Pavilion Publishing, Brighton.

Farmer E and Owen M (1995) *Child Protection Practice: Private Risks and Public Remedies.* HMSO, London.

Garbarino J (1982) *Children and Families in the Social Environment.* Aldine, New York.

Ghate D and Hazel N (forthcoming) *Parenting in poor environments: A national study of parents and stress.*

Gilligan R (2000) *Promoting Positive Outcomes for Children in Need: The Assessment of Protective Factors.* In Horwath J (ed) (2000) *The Child's World: Assessing Children in Need. The Reader.* The NSPCC, London.

Gorrell-Barnes G (1994) *Family Therapy.* In Rutter M, Taylor E and Hersov L (eds) *Child and Adolescent Psychiatry: Modern Approaches.* pp.946–967. Blackwell, London.

Haggerty R J, Sherrod L R, Garmezy N and Rutter M (1996) *Stress, Risk and Resilience in Children and Adolescents*. Cambridge University Press, Cambridge.

Hallett C (1995) *Inter-agency Co-ordination in Child Protection*. HMSO, London.

Hallett C and Stevenson O (1980) *Child Abuse: aspects of inter-professional co-operation*. Allen and Unwin, London.

Higham P (1999) *Reach Out – But will we be there?* In Community Care 29 April – 5 May 1999. pp.24–25.

Hill M, Laybourn A and Brown J (1996) Children whose parents misuse alcohol: a study of services and needs. *Child and Family Social Work*. **1**: 159–167.

Holman B (1998) *Faith in the Poor*. Lion Publishing, Oxford.

Home Office (1950) *Children neglected or ill-treated in their own homes*. Joint Circular with Ministry of Health and Ministry of Education.

Horwath J (ed) (2000) *The Child's World: Assessing Children in Need. The Reader*. The NSPCC, London.

Hudson B L (1991) *Behavioural Social Work*. In Lishman J (ed) *Handbook of Theory for Practice Teachers in Social Work*. Jessica Kingsley, London.

Hudson B, Hardy B, Henwood M and Wistow G (1999) In Pursuit of Inter-Agency Collaboration: What is the contribution of theory and research? *Public Management: an international journal of research and theory*. **1**(2): 235–260.

Hudson B (2000) *Inter-agency collaboration – a sceptical view*. In Brechin A, Brown H and Eby M A (eds) (2000) *Critical Practice in Health and Social Care*. The Open University/Sage, London.

Hunt J, McLeod A and Thomas C (1999) *The Last Resort*. The Stationery Office, London.

Iwaniec D (1996) *The Emotionally Abused and Neglected Child*. Wiley, Chichester.

Jack G (1997) An Ecological Approach to Social Work with Children and Families. *Child and Family Social Work*. **2**: 109–120.

Jackson S (1987) *The Education of Children in Care*. University of Bristol, School of Applied Social Studies, Bristol.

Jewitt C (1984) *Helping Children Cope with Separation and Loss*. Batsford/BAAF, London.

Jones D P H (1998) *The effectiveness of of intervention*. In Adcock M and White R (eds) (1998) *Significant Harm: its Management and Outcome*. pp.91–119. Significant Publications, Croydon.

Jones D and Ramchandani P (1999) *Child Sexual Abuse: Informing Practice from Research*. Radcliffe Medical Press. Abingdon.

Jones DPH, Newbold C and Byrne G (1999) *Management, Treatment and Outcomes*. In Eminson M and Posslethwaite R (eds) (1999) *Munchausen Syndrome by Proxy Handbook*. Butterworth/Heineman.

Katz A, Buchanan A and Ten Brinke J-A (1997) *The Can Do Girls – A Barometer of Change*. Department of Applied Social Studies and Research, Oxford.

Lawton D (1998) *The Number and Characteristics of Families with More than One Disabled Child.* Social Policy Research Unit, University of York.

Masten A and Coatsworth D (1998) Development of Competence in Favourable and Unfavourable Environments. *American Psychologist*, February 1998.

McAuley C (1999) *The Family Support Outcomes Study.* Home Start UK/ Northern Health and Social Services Board, Northern Ireland.

Maluccio A (ed) (1991) *Promoting Competence in Clients: a New/Old Approach to Social Work Practice.* The Free Press, New York.

Parton N (1987) *The Politics of Child Abuse.* Routledge, London.

Perry BD (1993) Neuro-development and the neuro-physiology of trauma. *The Advisor* **6**(**1**): 1, 14–18; **6**(**2**): 1, 14–20.

Pugh G (1999) *Parents under Stress.* Community Care, 2 –8 September 1999.

Reder P and Duncan S (1999) *Lost Innocents.* Routledge, London.

Reder P and Lucey C (1995) *Assessment of Parenting: Psychiatric and Psychological Contributions.* Routledge, London.

Rosenfeld A A, Bailey R, Siegal B and Bailey G (1986) Determining incestuous contact between parent and child: frequency of children touching parents' genitals in a non clinical population. *Journal of American Academy of Child Psychiatry.* **25**: 481–484.

Rushton A, Treseder J and Quinton D (1988) *New Parents for Older Children.* BAAF, London

Rutter M (1974) *Dimensions of Parenthood: some myths and some suggestions.* In Department of Health and Social Security (1974) *The Family in Society: dimensions of parenthood.* HMSO, London.

Rutter M and Rutter M (1992) *Developing Minds: Challenging and Continuity across the Life Span.* Penguin, Harmondsworth.

Rutter M (1996) Stress Research: Accomplishments and tasks ahead. In Haggerty R J et al (1996) *Stress, Risk and Resilience in Children and Adolescents.* pp.354–386. Cambridge University Press, Cambridge.

Rutter M (1999) Resilience concepts and findings: implications for family therapy. *Journal of Family Therapy.* **21**: 119–144, 159–160.

Schofield G (1998) Inner and outer worlds: a psychosocial framework for child and family social work. *Child and Family Social Work.* **3**: 57–67.

Schofield G and Brown K (1999) Being there: a family centre worker's role as a secure base for adolescent girls in crisis. *Child and Family Social Work.* **4**: 21–31.

Seden J (2000) *A Review of the Literature: Assessment in Social Work.* In Department of Health (2000b) *Studies which inform the development of the Framework for the Assessment of Children in Need and their Families.* The Stationery Office, London.

Seligman M E P (1975) *Helplessness: On Depression, Development and Death.* W H Freeman, San Francisco.

Shaw C (1998) *Remember my messages . . .* The Who Cares? Trust, London.

Sinclair R (1998) *The education of children in need.* Research in Practice/NCB, Dartington.

Siporin M (1975) *Introduction to Social Work Practice.* Macmillan, New York.

Skinner B R (1974) *About Behaviourism.* Cape, London.

Social Exclusion Unit (1998) *Bringing Britain Together: A National Strategy for Neighbourhood Renewal.* The Stationery Office, London.

Social Services Inspectorate (1999) *Getting Family Support Right. Inspection of the Delivery of Family Support Services.* Department of Health, London.

Stevenson O (1998) *Neglected Children: Issues and Dilemmas.* Blackwell Science, Oxford.

Thoburn J, Murdoch A and O'Brien A (1986) *Permanence in Child Care.* Basil Blackwell, Oxford.

Thoburn J, Wilding J and Watson J (2000) *Family Support in Cases of Emotional Maltreatment and Neglect.* The Stationery Office, London.

Thomas C and Beckford V (1999) *Adopted Children Speaking.* BAAF, London.

Tucker S, Tatum C and Frank J (1999) *The Experiences of Former Young Carers.* The Children's Society, London.

Tunstill J and Aldgate J (2000) *Services for Children In Need: From Policy to Practice.* The Stationery Office, London.

Utting D (1995) *Family and Parenthood: Supporting Families, Preventing Breakdown.* Joseph Rowntree Foundation, York.

Utting D (1996) *Reducing criminality among young people: A sample of relevant programmes in the United Kingdom.* Home Office, London.

Ward H (2000) *The Developmental Needs of Children: implications for assessment.* In Horwath J (ed) (2000) *The Child's World: Assessing Children in Need. The Reader.* The NSPCC, London.

White M and Epston D (1990) *Narrative Means to Therapeutic Ends.* Norton, New York.

# 2

# Assessing black children in need and their families

## Introduction

2.1 The population of England is comprised of many white minority ethnic groups as well as black minority ethnic groups and the differences in culture, religion, language and traditions for white minority ethnic groups have to be accounted for just as they do for black minority ethnic groups.

2.2 There are also a number of white minority ethnic groups who experience oppression on the basis of their ethnic, cultural or religious identity. In assessing families these experiences should be acknowledged and addressed.

2.3 This chapter focuses specifically on the needs of black children and families. Black here refers to children and families of Asian, African and Caribbean origin including children of dual heritage.

2.4 Whilst there are some similarities and parallels in the experiences of black and white minorities in Britain there is also a fundamental difference. Institutional racism has resulted in the significant impairment of the life opportunities of black people in this country (MacPherson, 1999).

2.5 Institutional racism operates within the field of child welfare. Over the last thirty years concern has been expressed about the number of black children in care (Batta, McCulloch and Smith, 1979; Adams, 1981; Rowe et al, 1989; Barn, 1993; 1997), the lack of take up of family support services (Butt and Box, 1998), and the lack of potential for some black children (London Borough of Lambeth, 1997; The Bridge Child Care Consultancy Services, 1991).

2.6 Assessing the developmental needs of children is a complex process which requires all relevant aspects of a child's life experience to be addressed. For black children assessments should address the impact that racism has on a particular child and family and ensure that the assessment process itself does not reinforce racism through racial or cultural stereotyping.

2.7 This chapter aims to assist child welfare professionals in undertaking assessments of black children in need and their families.

## Assessing black children in need and their families

2.8 Within the current context of practice, professionals charged with responsibilities for promoting the welfare of children and their families often struggle with how best to address the needs of black children and their families. Although many professionals are aware that it is essential to take account of race and culture, and in particular to be culturally sensitive in their practice, they are often at a loss to translate this into practical terms. In assessing the developmental needs of black children and their families practitioners should address two key questions:

- **What are the developmental needs of black children and their families, and in what ways are these similar, and in what ways do they differ from the developmental needs of white children and families?**

- **How can these developmental needs be responded to in work with black children and families?**

2.9   Both black and white children require their parents or carers to respond to their same fundamental care needs. They all need basic care, warmth, stimulation, guidance, boundaries and stability. Any child who grows up without access to these basic life blocks (as a result of poor parental care) will suffer to a greater or lesser extent.

2.10   The base lines for assessing parenting capacity and the child's developmental needs should be the same irrespective of whether a black or a white child is being assessed.

2.11   Later in this chapter, we look in detail at the similarities in and differences between the needs of black children and their families compared with white children and their families when using the Assessment Framework dimensions. Each of the three domains of the Assessment Framework will be addressed with respect to each of its dimensions.

2.12   Firstly, the context will be set for assessing black children and families. This includes their demographic and socio-economic situation and the changing nature of culture, as well as some key issues in professional practice.

## Demography

2.13   According to the 1991 census the total black and minority ethnic population of Britain is over 3 million people (5.5%). Of this 2.9 million black and minority ethnic people live in England, 59.5 thousand live in Scotland and 40.5 thousand live in Wales.

2.14   There are considerable regional variations in the ethnic composition of the population with the largest composition being in London at 44.8% and West Midlands, especially in Birmingham at 14% (Owen, 1992). Although there are regional variations in ethnic composition of the population, there are few areas where black people do not have a presence (Butt and Mirza, 1996).

2.15   One important feature of the black community is its relative youth compared to the white community. For instance adults aged over 45 constitute 39% of the white community compared to 18% of the black and minority ethnic community, and adults aged over 65 account for 16.9% of the white community and only 3.2% of the black and minority ethnic communities (Jones, 1993).

2.16   More importantly children under 15 constitute 33% of black and minority ethnic communities compared to 19 % in the white communities. In certain parts of the country such as the London Boroughs of Newham and Tower Hamlets children make up the majority of the population. Other important features of the population include:

- A very diverse black population with wide variations in class, countries of origin, socio-economic conditions, religion and languages;

- An increasing number of adult mixed relationships with 40% of African Caribbean men and 20% of African Caribbean women in mixed relationships (Berrington, 1996; Haskey, 1997). Importantly, 80% of black adults in mixed relationships are UK born and over half the children of mixed relationships are under the age of 15 (Haskey, 1997).

## Socio economic conditions

2.17 Evidence suggests that many of Britain's black population are experiencing economic hardship. According to the Social Exclusion Unit (1998) 'Ethnic minority groups are more likely than the rest of the population to live in poor areas, be unemployed, have low incomes, live in poor housing, have poor health and be the victims of crime'.

2.18 The important point about the socio-economic conditions of black communities from an assessment perspective is, as Butt and Mirza (1998) observe 'black communities are at greater risk of experiencing some of the stress so often associated with people who need the services of social care agencies'.

## The changing nature of culture for England's black population

2.19 The impact of social and economic forces, the effects of racism and racial harassment, changing family structures, access to suitable housing, the interaction between cultures, particularly in respect of children and young people and the experience of growing up in England are amongst a number of factors which have led to the changing nature of culture for black communities in this country. However, this has not led to an erosion of culture, as has sometimes been portrayed, but to the emergence of new cultural frameworks (Donald and Rattansi, 1992).

2.20 In some cases there has been a return to traditional values, exhibited by an increased interest in religious observance; in others, particularly among teenagers, there has been a mixing of cultures to create a street based culture strongly influenced by black, and in particular, black American and Caribbean culture.

2.21 Dosanjh and Ghuman (1998) describe the cross-fertilisation of cultures as 'enculturation' meaning:

This dynamic of enculturation...can be summarised as comprising a continuity with some traditional norms alongside the adopting of some of the norms of British lifestyles.

2.22 Despite these significant changes, culture remains a central part of the lives of black communities, for it is the primary way in which black communities can give meaning and continuity to their own distinct identities, rites, traditions, values, beliefs and customs. For many black people, it is their culture which gives them the strength to survive in a hostile environment.

# Key Issues in current child welfare practice

## Numbers of black children in care

2.23 There are no current available figures on the number of black children in care in England. There are a number of small scale and local studies which have indicated an over-representation of black children in care particularly of dual heritage and African Caribbean origin. Although there are difficulties in drawing conclusions from these studies on a national basis, their findings cannot be ignored.

2.24 Local authorities should analyse their population of children looked after to ascertain the extent to which the number of black children who are looked after reflects the local profile of the black population. If there is an under or an over representation of black children, the local authority should take active steps to identify the reasons for this situation and address it.

## Family Support

2.25 There is evidence also that black families are not gaining access to family support services. In a study of black families' use of family centres Butt and Box (1998) found that 13 out of the 84 centres had no black and minority ethnic users and 25 centres had black and minority ethnic users in equal proportion to their presence in the population. The authors conclude:

> Our study suggests that black communities do not always have access to family centres and rarely access the full range of services that are available. This is not merely an outcome of black families choosing which service they access (although there is an element of that) but that the services only rarely get black families through the front door and some black users appeared to be unaware of the range of services that were available.

## Inquiry Reports

2.26 At the same time, several Inquiry Reports into the deaths of black children provide evidence of a lack of intervention in situations where black children were at obvious risk of suffering significant harm from their parents. Two specific reports, *Whose Child? The Report of the Panel of Inquiry into the Death of Tyra Henry 1987* (London Borough of Lambeth, 1987) and *Sukina; An evaluation report of the circumstances leading to her death* (The Bridge Child Care Consultancy Services, 1991) make a direct link between racism and the practice of professionals when responding to the children and families concerned. Both reports identify that stereotyping of black families and a reluctance on the part of white professionals to intervene for fear of being accused of racism influenced practice.

2.27 It is clear that a more informed approach to the issue of race and culture within professional assessments is required. The remainder of this chapter will discuss ways in which professional practice could be developed to improve the assessment of and planning for black children and their families through an evidence-based, systematic and holistic approach to assessments with black families.

## Domain: Children's Developmental Needs

### Health

2.28 The following are some of the issues to be considered regarding health and black children and families:

- Research has shown the link between poverty and ill-health. Although this is as true for the white community as it is for the black community there is evidence to suggest that black and minority ethnic people experience poorer health. There are, however, differences amongst the different ethnic groups. A study by Nazroo (1997) found that on the whole Pakistanis and Bangladeshis reported the poorest health during assessments of general health, with Caribbeans having the next worst state of health;

- There is a very strong correlation between the physical health of children of all ages and adverse social and economic conditions. This is particularly apparent in the infant mortality rate, which is directly affected by factors such as economic status, type of accommodation, access to basic amenities and access to preventative and supportive health care. A number of studies have shown a higher infant mortality rate amongst poorer black communities, particularly within families from Bangladesh, Pakistan and the Caribbean (Smaje, 1999);

- There are some diseases which are more common amongst black and minority ethnic people and some which are particular to black communities only. In relation to the latter sickle cell disorder is one such illness, affecting mainly children from the African Caribbean community but may occur in people from India and Pakistan. For those affected by it, the most difficult aspect of the disorder is the pain experienced during the crisis. Symptoms can include infections such as meningitis as well as strokes (NHS Executive, 1998). Professionals working with black children affected by sickle cell can get more information about the disorder from the Sickle Cell Society;

- Particular groups of children such as refugee children can suffer post-traumatic stress syndrome. This can be directly attributed to the past experiences of many of the children. They may have witnessed death, violence and war prior to their arrival in the U.K.

---

### ➡ Pointers for Practice

Assessments of black families should take account of the specific health needs of different black communities and address:

- The extent to which the physical health of the child may be affected by adverse social conditions;

- The extent to which the child and family have direct access to appropriate advice support and services in relation to their health care needs;

- Whether the child or family members may be likely to suffer from sickle cell disorder;
- Whether past life experiences or trauma has had any affect on the physical health of the child.

## Education

2.29    From a psychological perspective, there is no difference in the cognitive or educational capacity or development of black children as compared to white. However, in social terms, there is no aspect of child development in which racism has had a greater impact in this country than that of educational and cognitive development.

2.30    Today, whilst there is an acknowledgement that there is no biological or genetic difference between black children's intelligence or educational ability as compared to white children, race continues to make a difference in the educational experience and achievements of black children. There is a great deal of evidence to suggest that black pupils in England under-achieve educationally and are more likely to be excluded from school than their white counterparts:

- The data on permanent school exclusions for 1996/97 show that African Caribbean pupils are more than four times as likely to face permanent exclusions compared to white pupils. Kundnani (1998) summaries evidence which suggests the 'profile of African Caribbean children who are excluded differs from that of excluded children generally; they are usually higher than average ability, exhibit less evidence of deep-seated trauma and are less likely to have shown disruptive behaviour from early in their school career'. Kundnani (1998) suggests that there is a problem 'between teachers and black children and that teachers' perceptions of black children (and vice versa) do, somehow play a crucial role';

- The over-representation of black children excluded from school has also been identified as an important issue by the Social Exclusion Unit;

- The most recent data on achievements in school show that African Caribbean, Pakistani and Bangladeshi children continue to under-achieve;

- Black parents consistently express concern about being undermined by the school system.

### ➡ Pointers for Practice

Assessment of black children's educational and cognitive development should take account of racism as it may manifest itself within the educational system and address:

- Whether the child has had the opportunity to realise their educational potential without the limitations imposed upon them by negative stereotyping;

- For an excluded child, the extent to which the exclusion is appropriate in relation to the child's behaviour;

- The extent to which the child's parents are consulted about and involved in the child's education.

## Identity and Emotional and Behavioural Development

2.31   Identity is important for all children: there are close links between the development of a child's identity and their emotional and behavioural development. Children who have emotional and behavioural difficulties often have a poor self-image and low self-esteem.

2.32   There is still considerable misunderstanding about the nature of identity and its central importance to all children. One of the reasons for this, is that identity is most often spoken about in relation to black children in situations where the child is perceived to be exhibiting identity problems. In fact, many children about whom there are professional concerns have problems with their identity, self-esteem and self-worth. These issues have been shown to be particularly significant for many children in the care system, both black and white. In their recent study of the effectiveness of care in childrens homes, Sinclair and Gibbs (1998) found that over 70% of children and young people had low self-esteem.

## The nature of Identity

2.33   Identity is difficult to define, yet it is central to every person's sense of their own individuality and place in society. Definitions range from spiritual or religious, through to psychodynamic, behavioural, social and structural interpretations. We will draw on the literature to propose a model of understanding identity in relation to black children and their families which is inclusive of all the elements of which it is comprised.

2.34   Within most societies, identity fulfils two useful functions. It allows individuals to understand and conceptualise themselves as distinct from others and it allows individuals to form group identities with other individuals who have similar characteristics to their own.

## Group identification

2.35   Group identification allows individuals to categorise each other in social interactions. Race, gender, class, disability, age, sexual identity, are all features of group identity which have an outcome for group members in terms of institutional discrimination and disadvantage. For black children and their families, being black in a white society is not just about personal or group identity, it is about a lived experience of discrimination on the grounds of colour and physical characteristics.

2.36   For children and young people who are both black and disabled, the experience of discrimination on the basis of their disability is compounded by the effects of racism. Despite this, many black and disabled children find that only one aspect of their experience is addressed at any one time.

## Individual and personal identity

2.37   Individual identity is the internal model which allows each person to have a perception of themselves as an individual and social being. We are all members of numerous social groupings, but we are also distinct in our own individuality from any other member of a given group to which we belong, despite some areas of commonality (See Erikson, 1968).

2.38 There is a complex interaction which takes place between the elements of one's personality to form an individual identity. Although each child is born with a specific genetic blueprint, inherited from their parents, each is unique. This is because each individual interaction between a child, his or her family, relationships, social context and environment, will be processed into an individual experience. These sets of individual experiences contribute towards the development of a whole personality.

2.39 Identity, therefore, has to be defined and assessed in terms of a holistic model of children's development which incorporates other facets of his or her developmental needs. The diagram below sets out how these key elements interact to form a child's identity (Figure 4).

2.40 From the time a child is born, he or she begins to develop an individual identity. First interactions with their carers, siblings and social contacts become part of the child's internal model of identity. These experiences also locate the child within a social world in which group identities begin to influence identity formation.

2.41 For black children and their families, racism affects both individual and group identities. Although there is no biological or genetic basis for the concept of a racial group, race has a social significance in that it affects the way in which a child him or herself and is perceived by others. A black child growing up within a predominantly white society will receive negative messages about being black, and needs a positive internal model of black identity to counteract negative stereotypes. A black child who is also disabled will be affected by their own and others perception of both their disability and their race, and will need to be given the opportunity to develop a positive sense of themselves which helps them to counteract negative messages about both.

## The Development of a racial identity

2.42 Racial identity is relevant to all children whether black or white. Being white is a racial identity, just as being black is one. However, because being white in England is often perceived as normative, being black becomes defined in terms of its difference to white norms. In fact, all children go through a developmental process of acquiring a racial identity, although many white adults and children along with a percentage of black adults and children are not aware they are doing so. Black children do not universally acquire a negative sense of self despite the effects of racism (Milner, 1983; Owusu-Bempah and Howitt, 1999).

2.43 The preconditions for identity formation for a secure black child growing up in a loving environment with racially aware black carers will be very different to the preconditions for a black child who has an insecure base, a poor caregiving environment and unaware or even hostile black or white carers.

2.44 For black children who do not have a positive sense of their racial identity, Cross (1971) provides one model for understanding and assessing racial identity. He explains the acquisition of their racial identity in terms of a five stage process:

- **Pre-encounter stage**
  This is before a child's has encountered racism, where their world view is influenced by a white perspective.

Figure 4 **A model of identity**

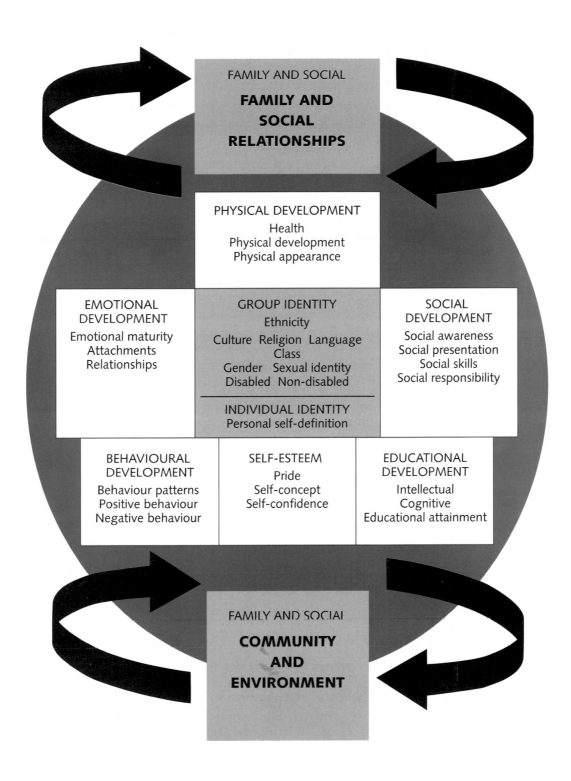

- **Encounter stage**

  This coincides with the child's first real encounter with racism. The significance of this experience forces the child to reconsider their previous world view and to reinterpret their experiences.

- **Immersion-emersion stage**

  This is where the child seeks to reject all previous aspects of their identity, and to become immersed in their blackness. However, this is only a superficial and reactive concept of black identity, which is more connected with the semblance of blackness, than with an integrated working model of a black identity. Individuals at this stage are often, wrongly perceived to have a positive black identity.

- **Internalisation stage**

  This is a move towards a more positive and integrated model of identity, in which an internal working model of black identity begins to take shape.

- **Internalisation-commitment stage**

  This is where the internal model links to aspects of a group identity, in that the child commits themselves to active participation in and commitment to the black community.

2.45   Cross' model also helps provide some insight into the links between personal racial identity and racial group identification. It helps us to understand the connections between personal racial identity, racial group identification and emotional and behavioural development. For instance a black person who group identifies as black, but is unable to internalise that identification will show in the way they behave the disconnections between their external and internal worlds. Similarly, a black child who has an integrated sense of their racial identity will exhibit this in their interactions and relationships with others.

2.46   For black children with one white parent (children of dual heritage) the connections between personal self-definition and group identification can hold particular significance. Although a number of recent studies have focused on the identity of children of dual heritage (Banks, 1992; Tizard and Phoenix, 1994; Katz, 1996), it should be stressed that these children should not be pathologised as having identity problems or identity conflicts. Many children of dual heritage have a very positive and integrated racial identity.

2.47   However, for some children of dual heritage, the dynamics of racial group identification are very complex. It is often stated that such children "want to be white" or are "denying their blackness". This is an over-simplification of their position.

2.48   For some of these children, particularly those who live with their white parent and have little or no contact with their black parent or the black parent's family, black self-definition means more than a journey towards self-recognition. For them there are emotional consequences to black racial group identification. If they perceive their white parent as caring and supportive, they may not wish to hurt a loved person by rejecting the white racial identity of their main carer, or white people in their main caregiving environment.

2.49   For these children it is important to understand the context in which the process of identity development is taking place. Working with these children and their white carers to strengthen the child's internal working model of racial identity is crucial to helping them feel positive about their racial identity and to deal with the racism which they will inevitably experience.

2.50 Whilst Cross' model was developed to help understand black racial identity, it is also applicable to the assessment of white racial identity. Just as the acquisition of an integrated sense of self in relation to race is a process for black people, so it is for white people. White children's attitudes to race reflect this. In their study of mainly white primary schools Troyna and Hatcher (1992) found that white children exhibited inconsistent attitudes towards race, ranging from overtly racist frameworks of interpretation through to well developed notions of race equality.

2.51 An interesting aspect of their research findings is the inconsistency between expressed values and behaviour:

> …a number of combinations of attitudes is possible, ranging from children who hold overtly racist beliefs but do not express them in behaviour, to children who hold racially egalitarian beliefs but use racist name calling in certain situations.

2.52 This demonstrates the need for dialogue about race and racism with white children and young people, as a way of exploring and integrating their notions of race. An awareness of the impact of racism and an understanding of their white cultural heritage are **also** important parts of positive identity development for white children in a multi-racial and multi-cultural society.

## Ethnicity

2.53 Whilst race is defined by heritage, colour, physical appearance, and physical characteristics, ethnicity is defined by geographic, political, historical, religious and cultural factors. Cashmore (1984) describes an ethnic group as:

> a group possessing some degree of coherence and solidarity composed of people who are, at least latently aware of having common origins and interests.

2.54 There are white ethnic groups as well as black ethnic groups. Minority status is related simply to being in the minority within a given population. Both black and white people continue to be oppressed and discriminated against on the basis of their ethnicity.

2.55 As an aspect of individual and group identity, ethnicity is significant in that it gives individuals a sense of community, heritage and belonging. Ethnicity, like race, cannot be acquired through lifestyle or association. As such, ethnicity is an important aspect of identity in both individual and group terms.

2.56 For children, the acquisition of an ethnic identity is an important process which helps them to connect their personal and family history to that of a community or social grouping. As such it gives them a sense of heritage.

## Cultural, religious and linguistic identity

2.57 Culture, religion and language are three distinct parts of identity which interconnect with racial and ethnic identity. However, they are distinct from both in that they can be acquired through the process of socialisation. A child can be born into a family from one cultural background, speak one language and be brought up with a particular set of religious beliefs. With a change of lifestyle, a new parental partnership, or a geographical move some or all of these aspects of the child's life may change, whilst their racial and ethnic identity remain the same.

2.58 However, culture, religion and language are very important aspects of group and individual identity. Whilst racial identity forms one important aspect of identity, individuals from the same racial group may have differences in terms of their cultural background, religious observance and linguistic identity.

## Culture

2.59 Much has been written about the concept of culture. We will not revisit old ground, but will summarise the following key points which are crucial to an understanding of the nature of culture and acquiring a cultural identity.

- Both black and white people have cultural identities;

- Culture is dynamic, not monolithic;

- Culture is acquired through live experiences;

- Culture is not static, but changes and develops over time;

- There are differences between families who have the same cultural background;

- Views of black cultures are influenced by cultural and racial stereotyping.

## The acquisition of cultural identity

2.60 Just as for racial identity, cultural identity functions at both a group and an individual level. It is acquired from live experiences. From birth, the child's senses are attuned to the specifics of their environment:

Individuation begins with the environment and evolves largely through sensory and perceptual experiences (Prohansky and Gottlieb, 1989).

2.61 The particular music young children hear, the language spoken or type of regional accent or dialect, the colours of clothing and fabrics seen, distinct household and cooking smells all provide a particular and distinct environment which contributes towards the formation of their cultural identity.

2.62 As a child grows older, interacts more with their family, community and the world at large, these interactions become more complex and multi-faceted. At the same time as developing capabilities for self-reflection and self-definition, the child acquires an individual cultural identity which has been shaped both by the particular context in which it has been developed and the child's own contribution to the process.

2.63 During this developmental process, the child will act and react in relation to a host of cultural information. Some of this will be specific to their own family traditions, some will be shared with individuals and families who come from a similar cultural background to the child. Through these interactions the child learns about individual family values and norms as well as about those norms and values which may be shared as group values.

2.64 For black disabled children there may also be other cultural connections which are important to them in addition to their family connections. For example, a black child who is deaf will also have experiences of deaf culture, where they may share commonalities with children and young people who have different ethnicities and family backgrounds to themselves. Whilst these commonalities will influence aspects of group-identification with other deaf children and young people, family culture will also be significant in defining identity. In this way, the acquisition of cultural identity can only be understood by taking account of the whole experience of each child or young person.

2.65 For some children, who do not grow up in an environment where they experience their own culture, perhaps because of being in substitute care, or because they do not have contact with any black family members, the acquisition of cultural identity is a more difficult process. For some of these children the only access to such experiences is through books or television programmes.

2.66 These sources of information can provide the child with information about cultural practices and traditions, but they cannot provide the child with a live and interactive experience in which the child has the opportunity to participate in and even shape events. Although useful if used appropriately, such information can also reinforce stereotypical and monolithic notions of culture because of its essentially static nature.

## Religion

2.67 Section 22(5)(c) of the Children Act 1989, requires local authorities to:

*give due consideration to… the child's religious persuasion…*

2.68 There is some evidence to suggest that information about the child's or family's religion is not always recorded in case files. Unpublished research undertaken by the authors in a city and county authority indicate that religion was not routinely recorded for black children.

2.69 Religion or spirituality is an issue for all families whether white or black. A family who do not practise a religion, or who are agnostic or atheists, may still have particular views about the spiritual upbringing and welfare of their children. For families where religion plays an important role in their lives, the significance of their religion will also be a vital part of their cultural traditions and beliefs (see CCETSW (1996) for a helpful training pack on Spirituality and Religion).

2.70 In research undertaken by Carl Hylton for the Moyenda Project in 1997, an issue that emerged strongly was the importance of spirituality as a survival strategy for black families living in England. The report says:

It is our intention to register strongly the concept of spirituality that came from all the respondents interviewed. Here, we are not particularly referring to religious adherence that forms a major aspect of the lives of many visual minority people. Spirituality as used here refers to wider feelings that include religious adherence, but is also concerned with a particular way of life encompassing strength, perseverance, forgiveness and the ability to build and concentrate on self-knowledge without posing the destruction of other ethnic groups.

## Language

2.71 The acquisition of language is central to any child's development. It is also a feature of the child's individual and group identity. The particular language, dialect or accent which the child learns and speaks will help them to define themselves, and others to define the child in relation to themselves.

2.72 For children and adults, language represents more than the ability to communicate. It also helps a child to access and be accessed by groups of people who share the same language, and to reinforce the child's sense of their own cultural group identity.

2.73 Dosanjh and Ghuman (1998) in their *Study of Child-rearing Practices of Two Generations of Punjabis* found that the mothers were keen to maintain religious rites and customs:

> Likewise, they are eager to teach their children their mother tongue, despite the lack of support from infant and primary schools.

2.74 It is vital that children have the opportunity to learn and maintain family languages. Although actual figures are not available, many children placed in long term substitute care have little or no opportunity to practise and develop their language skills apart from speaking English. For these children there can be no more poignant reminder of the loss of opportunity than the inability to communicate with other members of their own family and community in their own language.

2.75 This opportunity is particularly important for disabled children whose acquisition of language may be affected by their impairment.

## Social Presentation and Selfcare Skills

2.76 A child's social presentation and selfcare skills will reflect their own personal identity, their group affiliations and their upbringing and environment.

2.77 One of the indicators that a black child has an integrated sense of self as a black person is that they can define themselves in terms of their racial and cultural identity, as well as being self-confident about their physical appearance and characteristics.

2.78 However, some children do not grow up with any access to other black people. These children do not have the opportunity to naturally gain that support, strength and guidance in their everyday contact with black people.

2.79 For some black children who live with a black and a white parent their home is a very difficult environment in which to acquire a positive racial and cultural identity, because they experience racism from within their home or family. Some of these children internalise these negative feelings, and have very low self-esteem, whilst others may externalise their negative experiences into various forms of anti-social behaviour.

Identity allows individuals to understand and conceptualise themselves as distinct from others and allows individuals to form group identities with other individuals who have similar characteristics to their own. Race, culture, religion and language are central to group and individual identity. Assessments should to address identity holistically by considering:

- Any difficulties which the child may be having in acquiring a positive racial identity, and what help the child requires to enable them do so;

- The child's awareness of their own ethnicity and personal, family and community history. Where this is not available, what steps can be taken to obtain such information;

- The child's access to a lived experience of their culture, for example, attendance at a wedding, or participation in celebrations which include music, food and traditional rituals will give a child a far more profound and effective sense of their cultural identity than any amount of visual or written material;

- The religious and spiritual needs of black children and their families – this will require professionals to discuss the family's belief systems religion, rites and traditions and record them routinely;

- The identity of disabled black children holistically and not as a hierarchy of need, in that being black gives the child a specific perspective on their disability;

- The extent to which the child has the opportunity to learn about and maintain family languages. Where the child has not had this opportunity, what steps can be taken to address this deficiency;

- The extent to which a black disabled child has the opportunity to learn their first language. As some disabled children rely upon other forms of communication apart from the written or spoken word, it is vital that communication with their families is facilitated in a way that accounts for their own modes of communication as well as the family's first language. For example, the basis of British Sign Language is English. Translating BSL into English will facilitate the understanding of English speakers, but for those who speak other languages, further translation is required. Although the provision of interpreters is seen sometimes as a logistical nightmare for social welfare agencies, the ability to communicate and to be understood has to be promoted as a basic human right, without which any attempt at assessment would be impossible.

## Family and Social Relationships

2.80 Family and social relationships are central to all children's lives, whether they are black or white. For both white and black children their early experiences of parenting and social relationships can construct a blueprint for later social interactions.

2.81 When assessing parenting capacity and social relationships, practitioners often raise questions about the extent to which eurocentric models of child development are relevant to black families. Some think that using eurocentric theories such as attachment is not appropriate to the assessment of black families.

2.82    Attachments are central to all human societies, and there are no differences between black and white families in terms of the need for adults and children to form strong and positive relationships.

2.83    Children in all communities depend upon the specific care and attention of at least one significant adult who is able and willing to respond to the child's needs for both physical and emotional care. Children are vulnerable, particularly in their early years, and attachment to a significant adult fulfils a basic function to ensure their survival and wellbeing.

2.84    In the western world these parent-child relationships are explained by the theory of attachment, but in the popular culture of all societies the central importance of loving and protective relationships is represented in stories, folklore, poetry and music.

2.85    There is no difference in the preconditions for the formation of good attachments between black and white families. In both cases, attachments develop out of a relationship which is worked at by both baby and adult over a time. This relationship requires the participation of both parties, in that secure attachments are formed out of reciprocal relationships, in which there is a high degree of communication, matched responsiveness and consistency (Klaus and Kennel, 1976; Bowlby, 1988).

2.86    The third area of similarity is the importance of attachment to the internal working model which forms the basis for developing children's self-esteem, self-confidence and self-perception, as well as acting as a model for future social relationships and interactions (Bowlby, 1973). The theory is that through the care, responsiveness and affection that children receive from their attachment figures, they learn to see themselves as valued people who have a right to care and affection and who have self-worth. Children who grow up in environments where adult carers are not responsive to their needs, and are not caring or affectionate do not learn to see themselves as worthy of such love, and adapt their behaviour accordingly.

2.87    The basic concepts on which attachment theory is based are clearly applicable to all human relationships, and are important to our understanding of the human condition. However, there are aspects of attachment theory that require more discussion in relation to their applicability to black families.

2.88    The first of these is in relation to the identity of attachment figures. Much of the literature on attachment emphasises the importance of either the mother (Bowlby, 1969) and/or parents (Schaffer and Emerson, 1964; Rutter, 1972) as the main attachment figure for a child. It is here that there may be differences for some black families. Differences to family structures, communities and networks will play an important role in determining who the child will form key attachments with.

2.89    For many black families, family structures and interactions between family members are very different in nature and character to those of white nuclear families. Within this context a child may have strong attachments with a number of family members and adults who are not blood relatives of the family. Thomas (1995) refers to this as 'multiple attachments'. He says:

Friends and colleagues have talked about their experiences of being raised in

Bangladesh, Northern India and the Caribbean. They have talked about different cultural experiences of attachment. These have been varied, from having multiple mothering by grandmothers, mothers, aunts…This behaviour is thought to enable the small child to establish strong bonds with the extended family or clan which will be important for his or her future socialisation or welfare.

2.90    For many black families living in England, wider family networks and connections are important not just to the individual family, but to the survival of the whole community.

2.91    Social and economic circumstances have led to long term adult-child separations as a result of migration. Arnold (1975) highlighted particular issues of loss and separation for children who were parted from their parents as a result of migration to England, and the subsequent effects on attachments and relationships when family members were reunited having had little or no contact during the intervening years.

> The earlier the separation between mother and child in the Caribbean, the more problematic it became to re-establish bonds in the UK.

2.92    The impact of separation and loss is particularly acute for unaccompanied children and young people who are seeking asylum in this country. For these children, the losses, separations and traumas which they have experienced need to be understood within the context of attachments, separations and losses.

> These children have inevitably experienced significant disruption to their normal lives. All, whatever, their social background, will have suffered the trauma of losing familiar social landmarks, status and expectations (Social Services Inspectorate et al, 1995).

2.93    In such circumstances the existence of any family networks and connections are vital to the continued survival of individuals and communities. Owusu-Bempah and Howitt (1997) highlight the importance these connections have for children, citing the theory of socio-genealogical connectedness as a useful adjunct to attachment theory in understanding the nature of children's individual and group identities.

> The notion of socio-genealogical connectedness refers to the extent to which children identify with their natural parents' biological and social background. A basic tenet of this theory is that the degree to which children identify with their natural parent's backgrounds is dependent upon the amount and quality of information that they possess about their parents.

2.94    This echoes an earlier premise in this chapter, namely that children require positive information about their personal history and heritage in order to develop a sense of personal and group identity. For many black people, this connectedness also extends beyond individual families and into communities. Owusu-Bempah and Howitt (1997) explain:

> In a small-scale collective community where linkage may be with the whole group rather than to one's individual family, the information needed to achieve a sense of connectedness is readily available throughout the community, the child's sense of continuity is provided by the whole community rather than the individual parent of family.

**Pointers for Practice**

Information about family history and cultural heritage are vital not only to the child's sense of personal identity and wellbeing, but also to their sense of group identification. In assessing the child's relationships it is important to consider:

- The child's relationships within the context of their wider social networks and connections;

- The extent of quality and quantity of information the child has about their own roots and heritage, and how deficiencies in this information can be addressed;

- The specific family structure in which the child lives, and the patterns of attachment which operate within this particular black family including any attachment figures who may not be blood relatives;

- The impact of migration, separation and trauma on the child and wider family network.

## Domain: Parenting Capacity

### Basic Care

2.95   As stated earlier in this chapter, there are no differences in the basic care needs of black children compared to white children. For all children, their healthy development requires that basic care needs are responded to appropriately by the child's main caregivers.

### Ensuring Safety

2.96   Both black and white children have the same right and the same need to be protected from abuse, whether by acts of commission or omission. However, evidence cited at the beginning of this chapter, indicates that race plays a part in the protection of black children.

2.97   Whilst research studies have indicated that there is an over-representation of black children within the care system (see paragraph 2.23), there is also evidence that some black children are not being protected out of a fear on the part of white workers of being accused of racist practice.

2.98   *Whose Child? The Report of the Panel of Inquiry into the death of Tyra Henry 1987* (London Borough of Lambeth, 1987), a black child, suggested that the lack of support provided by the Social Services Department to help the child's grandmother care for her was influenced by gender based racial stereotyping. An over-idealised view of African-Caribbean women was cited as influencing social work practice with the family. As a result of this lack of support, Tyra returned home to her parents where she was subsequently killed by her step-father.

> There is a "positive", but nevertheless false stereotype in white British society of the Afro-Caribbean mother figure as endlessly resourceful ... essentially unsinkable. It may have been an unarticulated and unconscious sense that a woman like Beatrice

Henry would find a way to cope no matter what, that underlay the neglect of social services to make adequate provision for her taking responsibility for Tyra (London Borough of Lambeth, 1987).

2.99 In the case of Sukina Hammond, a child of mixed parentage who was killed by her father, the report of the circumstances leading to her death (The Bridge Child Care Consultancy, 1991) states:

> We know that agencies that are moving towards trying to be more sensitive and understanding to the racial and cultural needs of their client group, do risk failing to recognise the particular needs of an individual child. In addition, white professionals who have undergone anti-racist training can sometimes over-compensate out of fear of being accused of racism.

2.100 Studies (see Finkelhor, 1986; Jones and McCurdy, 1992) have shown little difference in rates of physical abuse, sexual abuse and neglect across different ethnic and racial groups. Despite this, there is evidence of differences in referral rates in relation to specific types of abuse for particular black ethnic groups.

2.101 In their study, *Operating the child protection system*, Gibbons, Conroy and Bell (1995) state that Black and Asian families were over-represented among referrals for physical injury (58% versus 42%) and under-represented referrals for sexual abuse (20% versus 31%) compared to white families. They conclude that:

> This illustrates cultural differences in child rearing and the difficulty of deciding what forms of physical punishment are "acceptable" in Britain.

2.102 Thoburn et al (1995) echo this concern in their research on family involvement in the child protection process:

> Disagreements about the appropriateness of physical punishment features in a disproportionate number of cases involving black families.

2.103 Farmer and Owen (1995) also refer to this dilemma in *Private Risks and Public Remedies*:

> In spite of (or perhaps because of) considerable sensitivity in their perceptions, a few workers were somewhat overwhelmed by the number of factors which appeared to be relevant in minority ethnic cases and they had difficulty in combining them, especially if culture, race and ethnicity were seen not as the total context for intervention but to be added at the end of a lengthening list.

2.104 It is evident that race features at every stage of intervention, from the point of referral onwards. An example of this is the differential referral rate for black families in relation to physical injury and sexual abuse in Gibbons, Conroy and Bell's study. The referral rate is not illustrative of the actual incidence of abuse within a given community, but it is indicative of which cases are referred to statutory agencies. It is erroneous to assume that there is less sexual abuse within the black community, as this perpetuates myths which results in sexual abuse being unrecognised and undetected within black communities.

2.105 It is equally inaccurate to assume that the referral rates for physical injury of children are based on different levels of physical chastisement within black communities, and it perpetuates another myth that physical abuse is cultural within black communities.

2.106 Whilst physical injury and physical punishment are often discussed as interchangeable terms there is a distinction between physically injuring a child and using forms of physical disciplines – such as smacking.

2.107 Within current debates on parenting the acceptability of smacking is a hotly debated topic. There are very different views held by parents about this both within and across cultural boundaries. Just as many black families may strongly support the use of smacking as a form of discipline so do many white families. Equally there are black as well as white families who are strongly opposed to smacking children.

2.108 Physical injury to children occurs in black families just as it does within white families, but it is not more or less a part of black culture than of white culture. Physical abuse is unacceptable whatever the context. If physical abuse was a part of black culture then all black children would be unsafe within black communities.

2.109 When a child is abused in a family, it is important to establish the circumstances in which the abuse took place, as a means of targeting areas for intervention to change patterns of behaviour. If it is assumed that the abuse occurs as a result of cultural patterns of behaviour, then the focus for intervention may be the culture itself.

2.110 Culture does not explain abuse. A parent who has injured a child may say "It is my culture to punish my child in this way". However, this does not explain why many other parents from the same culture do not punish their child using this level of physical chastisement, and some parents from the same culture use no physical punishment at all.

2.111 Culture can explain the context in which abuse takes place, it can explain the values, beliefs or attitudes of a parent at the time when an abusive incident took place, but it cannot provide an explanation for the parent's action in response to those values, beliefs or attitudes.

---

### Pointers for Practice

Issues of race and culture cannot simply be added to a list for separate consideration during an assessment. They are integral to the assessment process. In undertaking assessments of black families professionals should be mindful that:

- From referral through to core assessment, intervention and planning, race and culture have to be addressed using the Assessment Framework;

- Culture can explain the context in which an abusive incident took place, but not the behaviour or action of an individual parent. For example, a parent who injures their child with a belt may say that this form of punishment is "cultural". Their cultural context may explain the parents anger within the expectations that he or she has of the child, but will not explain why the parent acted upon this anger by using a belt to hit the child. Other parents from the same culture in a similar context may choose to punish the child without recourse to any physical punishment at all;

- Racial and cultural stereotyping of black families can led to inappropriate interventions in families as well as a failure to protect black children from abuse.

---

## Racial abuse and harassment

2.112 An area of abuse of black children, not generally addressed by the social work profession, is racial abuse and harassment. According to Dutt and Phillips (1996):

> Racial abuse and harassment on the whole received a 'no-reaction' response from social work professionals. Although many social services departments have developed policies on racial attacks and harassment, there is little evidence to suggest that the issue of racial abuse is a priority for departments or that practice is beginning to take into account the reality of racial abuse.

2.113 A review of research on racism and racial abuse undertaken by the NSPCC (Barter, 1999) highlighted a dearth of research on racial abuse of children and young people. It identified some important issues in this area namely:

- Racism and racial bullying are commonplace in the lives of minority ethnic children and young people, and in the lives of white children who will frequently witness racial bullying as bystanders;

- Studies focusing on racial bullying show that, compared to overall bullying figures, children from ethnic minorities are more likely to experience bullying than their white counterparts;

- The most common expression of racism is through racist name-calling, which research shows is often viewed by adults as trivial, although studies indicate that its impact on children can be profound;

- Although research evidence is limited, that available suggests racial bullying frequently involves the use of violence.

2.114 Although this review highlights the lack of material on the racial abuse and its impact on black disabled children, it quotes some studies specifically looking at racial abuse and black disabled people. One example is a small study undertaken by Begum (1992) on Asian disabled people and their carers. Her study shows that 'overall about half of the total sample reported that they had experienced racial harassment. Half of the disabled people had experienced some form of verbal abuse, and 14% reported racial violence'.

2.115 Whatever form racial abuse takes, the impact of the abuse is devastating for the child/young person, as well as for their family. The Childline study (1996) *Children and Racism* highlights some of the impact of racial abuse on children. The study states that 'racist bullying causes real suffering, effects children's self-esteem and confidence and renders some children and young people so despondent that they feel suicidal and attempt suicide'. The report concludes 'youngsters cannot deal with bullying on their own, they need adult help'.

2.116 Racial abuse may be a feature of the lives of black children of dual heritage living in predominantly white families. In their study of race and racism in the lives of young people of mixed heritage, Tizzard and Phoenix (1994) found that half the young people in the sample 'perceived either a parent or a sibling as being to some degree racially prejudiced'.

2.117 The Childline study also highlighted racism experienced by children in their own families. Comments from children calling Childline include:

*Mum has left because dad was hitting her. Now he's hitting me and calling me 'half-breed' and 'nigger' because my mum is black.*

*I am black and my mum is white...she has a new boyfriend who is completely racist... He is not nice to me. When we are alone...He says things like "you need a bath". This 12 year old girl felt she could not tell her mother because she wouldn't believe her.*

2.118 The Childline report concludes that 'perhaps the most unhappy children we hear from are those where racism is part of their family life. They are being excluded or abused by the people they love'.

---

 **Pointers for Practice**

Racial abuse damages children both physically and emotionally and as such warrants professional intervention to address the effects of this form of abuse whether it comes from within or outside the family. Assessments should consider:

- Whether racial abuse, racial bullying or racial violence impacts on the child or on the wider family;

- The extent of support, advice and intervention offered to the family, or the family require, and how this can be provided.

---

## Emotional Warmth

2.119 For all children emotional warmth is an essential prerequisite for healthy emotional development. But how is emotional warmth demonstrated, and to what extent do cultural variations exist in relation to demonstrating it?

2.120 Much of the literature on emotional abuse and neglect emphasises the absence of emotional warmth as one indicator of emotional abuse. Hoghhughi and Speight (1998) emphasise the importance of love, care and commitment to healthy emotional development:

Children need to feel they are loved consistently and unconditionally.

2.121 In *Beyond Blame, Child Abuse Tragedies Revisited,* Reder et al (1993) state:

The child must be wanted and treated as a person in his/her own right, whose feelings are respected and of concern to the parent. In order to provide such care, the parents must be able to put the child's needs above their own and tolerate the child's dependency and immaturity.

2.122 This represents an important base line for the assessment of emotional warmth. Parents or carers who are unable or unwilling to respond to the child's need for unconditional love and affection will not be able to meet one of the child's basic developmental needs.

2.123 All cultures recognise the need for affectionate relationships between adults and children, just as all cultures create social structures in which these relationships can develop. There are no differences between cultural groupings in this respect. But where differences do emerge is in the way in which this emotional warmth is demonstrated.

2.124 The demonstration of emotional warmth is also dependent upon rules in a family or community about physical contact. In some communities, there are more structured rules about male-female contact than in white English families, but this does not mean that everyone from that community will behave in exactly the same way in relation to demonstrating physical affection to children.

2.125 Differences in what constitutes valued social behaviour also creates variations. For example, in western societies emphasis is placed upon children learning the distinction between social time with family members and time alone such as at bedtime. As a result, western bedtime routines encourage children to sleep alone from quite early ages (Swanick, 1996).

2.126 If separate sleeping is not considered to be such a desired form of child behaviour, attempts by parents to impose such a pattern onto a child would be considered rigid and inflexible parenting. On the other hand, for parents who value the independence of separate sleeping arrangements, shared sleeping may be perceived as inappropriate and lacking boundaries.

2.127 Over time variations also occur within and between cultures. Fashions in child rearing practices have a strong influence in the way in which parents are expected to relate to children. At one time in England within certain white communities it was common practice to leave babies outside in prams during the day. Today this practice would be seen as neglectful. The practice of baby massaging, common in many black societies, was for many years considered to be undesirable and even abusive to children; now there are classes run by health professionals on baby massage.

2.128 The rise of the child care expert in western societies has exacerbated trends in parenting. Whereas parents traditionally learnt parenting skills from their own experience of being parented, today's parents are required to have a greater level of knowledge and skills in parenting.

### Pointers for Practice

There are differences in the way in which affection and love are shown to children by adults. Some of these will be based on established cultural patterns of behaviour whilst some will be related more to individual, family or social influences. In assessing emotional warmth:

- Assessments should take account of such variations, whilst still maintaining consistency in the application of minimum standards of child care;

- Professionals need to ensure that base lines are consistent across cultures. It is not acceptable that parents who demonstrate cold and unloving responses to children are able to justify their behaviour on the grounds of cultural differences;

- In an extended family or clan family structure the whole family may participate in the parenting of the child, including providing emotional warmth for the child. The parent–child interaction will only be one of many adult–child, child–child interactions which should be addressed in an assessment.

### Stimulation

2.129 Just as for emotional warmth, all children require stimulation, and just as for emotional warmth, the indicators for the presence of appropriate stimulation in an adult–child relationship have to be understood within a social and cultural context.

2.130 There are a number of myths about stimulation in black families which still have an impact on professionals today. The two key myths are:

- That Asian parents do not have toys to stimulate children;

- That black parents expect children to behave as mini-adults, and take on inappropriate responsibilities for household tasks.

2.131 The myth that Asian parents do not have toys for children seems to have been based upon the observations of some child care professionals that certain Asian families did not have play equipment in their homes.

2.132 For some Asian and Caribbean families in past generations, purchased toys were in evidence, but were not the main focus of play activity. Particularly for those families who came from rural parts of India or the Caribbean, game playing took place outdoors, and play equipment consisted of whatever was available in the fields and woods where the play took place. The same was true for many white families who grew up in similar environments in England. In a move to a colder, urban environment, the opportunity for outdoor play was severely curtailed. Children were unable to create their own games and exploration became supervised and controlled. Play thus became a more organised and contained activity. Within this context families also adapted to their changed environment, and toys have become the main focus for play for all children whether black or white.

---

 **Pointers for Practice**

- In assessing stimulation in black families it is important to recognise that children's learning may be encouraged in a range of ways, and that the trappings of a stimulating environment, such as toys and play equipment are not guarantors of a stimulating environment for children. In assessing families workers should make sense of different practices.

- In western societies the concept of childhood is underpinned by the desire to be free of adult responsibilities and to have opportunities for explanation, learning and play. In many black families children are not expected to take on adult responsibilities, but they are expected to learn certain skills that will prepare them for adult life. Whilst western values encourage pretend play, many black families take pride in teaching children the basics of cooking and child care at quite young ages.

---

### Guidance, Boundaries and Stability

2.133 Currently, guidance and boundaries is perhaps the most conflictual area of parenting for many black parents. It is also the area in which many black families seek stability in a changing world, through the maintenance of traditional values.

2.134 There are inherent tensions created by trying to maintain a strong sense of black culture and heritage, whilst at the same time living in an industrialised western and racist environment with very different values from the traditions of Africa, the Caribbean or Asia.

2.135 Black parents recognise and worry about these tensions:

> Along with trends in the wider UK population, there appears to be a trend among black families towards an emphasis on co-operation rather than the discipline of physical control... This has been assisted by changes to UK statutes, which some Black parents view as very child-centred, and also as a double-edged sword (Hylton, 1997).

2.136 Black parents wish to imbue their children with the values which they hope will help their children to survive in a hostile environment, but they are concerned that their values do not have the support of many professionals.

> Black parents often find that what is being reinforced at home varies greatly from at school, so both child and parent are in a dilemma regarding support for what they value within their culture (Grant, 1996).

2.137 At the heart of the value conflict between black and white western values lies different perspectives on independence.

> In non-Western European extended families, autonomy and competence are differently defined. There is more likely to be an emphasis on parents raising children to be "dependable" – that is to take on a role within the extended family, rather than be independent. This can cause much friction in the home for children who have grown up within western society (Grant, 1996).

2.138 Dosanjh and Ghuman's study (1998) confirms the desire of many Asian parents to maintain traditional values:

> From the responses of the Punjabi mothers of both generations we infer that they are in favour of encouraging their children to be conscious of, and to appreciate, the custom of familial interdependence rather than to follow and absorb the Euro-American style of rugged individualism.

2.139 This is essential if professionals are to gain the support of black families as partners in the protection of black children. Black families at present perceive child welfare professionals as undermining of black communities. In Hylton's study, one black parent speaks for many:

> (UK) society is destroying the black family in the sense that the very same society that said to you, you cannot scold your children, you cannot speak too roughly to your children, will take your child away from you and put your child in a social environment … so that the values that they pass down to your children are worse than what you would give … and it's the same society that would pick up your child that they took away from you in the first place, and put your child behind bars, and say he's a criminal.

**Pointers for Practice**

In assessing guidance and boundaries, professionals should understand the context in which these are developed. In undertaking assessments:

- Professionals should be aware that black families at present perceive child welfare professionals as undermining of black communities, particularly in relation to the guidance of and boundaries for young people;

- The imposition of a western and individualised model of autonomy and independence is at variance with the values of many black families, and it's application in assessment and intervention can destabilise families and family support networks;

- Where intergenerational or family conflicts arise in relation to guidance and boundaries, negotiations are necessary to reconcile differences.

## Domain: Family And Environmental Factors

2.140 Social work with children and families is, as Macdonald (1991) acknowledges 'rooted in the pain and suffering of people who are struggling against odds which are sometimes too great, whether that is due to illness, poverty, racism, homelessness or other strains and pressures'.

2.141 Any assessment that ignores the wider context of social and economic factors and its impact on family life, is incomplete as is one which further ignores racism and its impact on the social and economic context of black families.

2.142 This section draws on research and other evidence to highlight some of the issues pertinent to black families regarding family and environmental factors. This information sets out the wider socio-economic context of black families. The general issues may or may not all be relevant to each family and even where it is relevant will not affect all families in the same way.

**Pointers for Practice**

- Each of the dimensions identified should not be seen in isolation from each other. For instance, having a large family may not in itself be a problem for any one family but if the family are also experiencing overcrowding and low income it may result in family members experiencing additional stress. Any assessment process should take account of the impact on the family of the various factors interacting with each other.

### Family History and Functioning

### Family size

2.143 An analysis of the 1991 census shows (Haskey, 1997):

- of every thousand Black Caribbean families, 540 are families with children;

- for the Pakistani community this figure is 810 per thousand families;

- and 840 out of every thousand families for the Bangladeshi community;

- The comparative figure for white communities is 417 per thousand families.

2.144 There are some differences in the family sizes of different black communities. A recent survey (PSI, 1997) shows, for instance, that Pakistani and Bangladeshi people have larger families with 33% and 42% of them respectively having four or more children. In comparison, in Caribbean communities the percentage of families with four or more children is 7%, in Indian families 11% and in Chinese and African-Asian families 3%.

2.145 As Butt and Mizra (1996) conclude 'For the vast majority of black communities, family units with children under the age of 16 are a common experience. Furthermore, these families are likely to have more children under the age of 16 than their white counterparts'.

## Family structure and arrangements

2.146 Butt and Box (1998) observe that public debate on families 'often conflates marital status and the actual living arrangements of families, and on occasion unmarried mothers and lone parents are seen as interchangeable'. The 1991 census has allowed both issues to be explored. In relation to marital status, the data shows that whilst over 66% of India, Pakistani and Bangladeshi men over 16 are married, over 47% of Caribbean men over the age of 16 are single. In relation to different family types, the census analysis also shows that whilst 55% of Caribbean families with children under 16 are lone parents, 92% of Indian families with children under 16 are married couple families (Haskey, 1997).

2.147 The ONS (1996) suggests:

- around 54% of black Caribbean children are brought up in lone mother households and 3% in lone father households;

- for children of Indian origin around 7% are in lone mother households and around 1% in lone father households;

- for Pakistani and Bangladeshi communities the figures are 8% in lone mother and 1% in lone father households;

- for the Chinese community 11% of children are being brought up on lone mother and 1% in lone father households.

2.148 Regarding family structures for children in the 'Black other' category, the ONS (1996) figures suggest that 49% of children categorised as 'Black other' live in lone mother households and 2% live in lone father households. Two separate studies (Barn, 1993; Barn et al, 1997) also show that the majority of looked after children of dual heritage in these studies had a white mother and the majority of their parents had never married.

**Pointers for Practice**

- In assessing black families it is important to take account of family size and structure. For instance, a family with three or more children with a low income and poor housing is a family likely to experience hardship. Any assessment process should address the implications of this for families;

- Although the fact of a lone parent household in itself may not be an issue for an individual family, a lone parent household with no support networks may impact on family functioning. Furthermore, lone parenthood can have an impact on income and wealth, and in turn can impact on the material wellbeing of children. This should be taken account of in an assessment.

- In relation to a child of dual heritage assessments should consider the implications of family arrangements on the child and family. For instance how does living in a white only household impact on the child's position within the family, or how does a single white mother's isolation from her community affect her relationship with her child?

- It is important for assessors to understand that the evidence of a higher incidence of lone parenthood amongst Caribbean people does not rule out exploration of the issue of 'visiting' relationships, where the responsibility for care of the children may be shared although the parents may not live together.

## Parenting strengths and difficulties

2.149 Despite the social and economic impact of racism on families and the detrimental impact of immigration laws and racial violence on families and communities, over many generations black families have demonstrated strengths and resilience in the face of adversity. Unfortunately social work practice with black families has often failed to work with the strengths of black families and has relied instead on a problem oriented approach to black families.

2.150 A deficit model which views families as dysfunctional can preclude adequate support being provided to families. For instance, evidence shows that where professionals fail to provide adequate support in the early stages of intervention there is an increased likelihood of the child becoming looked after (Barn, 1993).

2.151 It is also apparent that race is a factor in the support offered to black families. Many black families do not access family support services (Butt and Box, 1998) and the Tyra Henry and Sukina Hammond Inquiry Reports demonstrate that racism and gender based stereotyping can impact on the amount and timing of the support which is offered.

 **Pointers for Practice**

- Assessments should inform interventions which build on the strengths of black families, whilst ensuring that areas of difficulty or potential risk to the child's safety are identified and addressed appropriately;

- An empowerment model of assessment should recognise the life experiences of black families, particularly the ability of families to survive and resist a system that is disadvantaging;

64

- Targeted support to address family problems should be based on an understanding of a family's circumstances as the result of the assessment process rather than on the basis of assumptions underpinned by stereotypical beliefs of black families.

### Wider Family

2.152 The wider family, often referred to as the extended family, has been an important feature of the lives of many black and minority ethnic people. Hylton (1997) notes, in his study of the survival strategies used by black families, that the majority of black people 'rarely made a disconnection between the unit of mother, father and child – the so called nuclear family – and relatives such as grandparents, sisters, brothers, aunts and uncles. They were all collectively known as the "family"'.

2.153 For many, the wider family is not restricted to aunts, uncles and grandparents, but as has already been highlighted earlier, includes family friends and other non-blood relatives.

2.154 However, not all individual black families will have this wide family network. This is of particular relevance for many refugee and asylum seeking individuals and families who have left their homeland alone or with their immediate family. For these people, in common with other black people, the family in the wider sense is central. Family in this context could be other refugees and asylum seekers, and links will therefore be made with individuals and families coming from the same geographical regions.

2.155 For some families with no close family members in this country, links with family and friends living either in their country of origin or other parts of the world, will be important.

### Pointers for Practice

- In assessing black families, practitioners should ascertain from children and family members their perception of who constitutes their wider family and tap into the strengths that may be present in that wider family network.

### Housing

2.156 Butt and Mirza (1996) in reviewing the research data on housing and tenure for black communities conclude 'Though a large proportion of black people own their own accommodation there is evidence to suggest that the black community occupy older inner city accommodation which lacks basic amenities. Furthermore, black households are more likely to experience overcrowding compared to the white population'.

2.157 There is some evidence to suggest black people live in neighbourhoods that are rundown. A survey (PSI, 1997) found:

> Ethnic minorities tended to live in areas with higher than average levels of unemployment, they were more likely than whites to mention environmental problems such as graffiti, vandalism and vermin infestation, and they were more likely than whites to report problems of personal and property crime and nuisance trouble from some young people.

Overall, whites were the most likely to say they were very satisfied with the current neighbourhoods and housing: Caribbean, Bangladeshi's and the Chinese were the most likely to be dissatisfied with their local neighbourhoods, and Caribbeans and Bangladeshi's were the most dissatisfied with their neighbourhoods.

## Employment

2.158 The same PSI Survey (1997) found also that unemployment rates amongst men under retirement age was the highest amongst Caribbean (31%) Bangladeshi (42%) and Pakistani men (38%). The unemployment rates amongst Chinese, African Asians and Indians was 9, 14 and 19 % respectively. In relation to the white community the percentage is 15.

2.159 For women the Chinese had the lowest rates of unemployment at 6% followed by whites at 9%, African Asians and Indians 12% and Caribbeans at 18 %. For Pakistani and Bangladeshi women it was 39% and 40% respectively.

## Income

Poverty is more than simply economic deprivation, it means being completely isolated from the means to change one's circumstances (Carter, 1998).

2.160 The extent of poverty in black communities is now well documented. Berthoud, in analysing data from the fourth national survey of ethnic minorities in Britain which was conducted by PSI/SCPR in 1994, notes that 82% of Pakistani, 84% of Bangladeshi, 45% of Indians, 41% of Caribbean and 39% of 'African Asian' households had incomes that were below half the average income, in comparison to 28% of white households.

2.161 The PSI survey (1997) notes that although there were wide variations in the extent of poverty in the various black communities, 'all minorities included in this survey, with the exception of people of Chinese origin, were disadvantaged with respect to the white majority'.

2.162 The survey found also that:

- the extent of poverty among both Pakistani and Bangladeshi households was outstanding;

- Caribbean, Indian and African Asian households were more likely to be in poverty, and less likely to have relatively high family incomes than white households;

- where financial problems such as arrears and money worries were concerned, Caribbeans had exceptionally high levels of rent arrears and were much more likely to report money worries than any other group.

2.163 No specific information exists about the level and extent of poverty and its impact on black disabled children and their families. Evidence suggests, however, that families with a disabled child are generally affected significantly by poverty. A national survey

(Beresford, 1995) exploring the needs and circumstances of families caring for a severely disabled child found that families in the survey 'had substantially lower incomes than the general population...'. The survey **also** shows that employment levels for mothers of disabled children were much lower than **for** mothers with non-disabled children and that 'nine out of ten lone parent families, and a third of two parent families, had no income other than benefits'.

2.164 Although there are no data available on black children who are disabled the incidence and prevalence of disability amongst black communities is likely to be either the same rate and certainly no less than in the white population (Butt and Mirza, 1996). Given that family units with children are the rule rather than the exception and the disproportionate levels of poverty in the black communities, it could be safely concluded that black disabled children are as likely to experience poverty as white disabled children.

---

 **Pointers for Practice**

- In assessing the needs of children and their families it is important to understand the implications of social and economic context within which families live and more importantly how fears and worries about money, health, education and employment impact on family life;

- In assessing black families any attempts to disregard the impact of racism on the social and economic context in which black families live will result in an assessment which is incomplete.

---

### Families Social Integration

2.165 The extent to which individual black families feel integrated and part of their local neighbourhood will vary. The following factors might have an impact on the social integration of black family's into their neighbourhoods:

- Black families tend to live in areas of higher than average black population. This is as much to do with individuals and families choosing to be in surroundings and with people who appear familiar, as it is to do with people feeling 'safe in numbers'. For many black people living amongst a majority of black people gives them a sense of belonging and provides them with a certain level of support and security;

- Black communities are not homogeneous. Some black families, although living in predominantly black areas, may be in cultural or religious minorities in those communities. This will not, in itself, be problematic but individual families from those minority groups may find their support network is located outside their locality. For instance, refugee families may consider support from other refugee families more appropriate. Their social integration into their locality may be less important than their social and emotional links with other refugees;

- Many black families live in hostile communities where racial abuse and harassment are a daily feature of their lives. There are some areas where black families are frightened to allow their children to play outside home and where adults feel under siege.

---

**⟶ Pointers for Practice**

- Any assessment with individual black families should recognise that although many black families gain strength from living amongst their own community, there are individual black families whose experience of living amongst black people may not necessarily be a positive one. As with the white community, the reasons for any black family feeling either isolated or ostracised from the majority community will vary. Whatever the reason it is important to think of the support networks for such families;

- Alongside the individual impact which racial abuse and bullying has on children, it is important to consider the impact of racial violence on communities. Fear of abuse or attacks can affect whole ways of life in particular communities which are targeted for such treatment by reducing the freedom of movement of women, children and older people in both the hours of daylight and at night. In such cases local authorities should plan for community safety in a more pro-active and co-ordinated way, using the auspices of children's planning processes and area child protection committees, alongside initiatives to reduce crime and improve safety in the locality.

---

### Community Resources

2.166 The anomalous situation regarding community resources for black communities is that on one hand black individuals have access to some very positive support from black voluntary organisations and on the other have little access to resources provided by the statutory sector and some white voluntary sector organisations.

2.167 In relation to preventative services for children and families provided by statutory organisations, evidence suggests that black families have less access to those services than white families. For instance in relation to child protection a study by Farmer and Owen (1995) found that 'many black families did not have access to much needed services. Even after registration this situation often continues, partly because of lack of appropriate resources'.

2.168 Equally, a study of family centres and their use by black families also found that 'family centres are not intrinsically providers of accessible and appropriate services to black families' (Butt and Box, 1998).

2.169 Although services from mainstream organisations have been inaccessible black communities have had some very positive support from black voluntary organisations. The role of the black voluntary sector in providing much of needed services to black people is well recognised (Phaure, 1991; Atkin, 1996; Butt and Box, 1998). Apart from providing much needed services, involvement in black organisations has also been one of the survival strategies used by many in the black communities (Hylton, 1997).

**Pointers for Practice**

- During the assessment process professionals should ascertain from families what are their perceptions of available community resources what kinds of services would be most helpful to them and how to make statutory sector services appropriate and accessible to them.

# References – Chapter 2

Adams N (1981) *Lambeth Directorate of Social Services.* London Borough of Lambeth.

Arnold E (1975) *Out of sight not out of mind.* M.Phil, University of Sussex.

Atkin K (1996) An opportunity for change, voluntary sector provision in a mixed economy of care. *Race and Community Care.* Open University Press.

Banks N (1992) Some considerations of racial identification when working with mixed ethnicity children and their mothers as social services clients. *Child Development.* **41**: 49–67.

Barn R (1990) Black children in local authority care; admission patterns. *New Community.* **16**(2): 229–246.

Barn R (1993) *Black Children in the Public Care System.* Batsford, London.

Barn R (1999) White Mothers, Mixed Parentage Children and Child Welfare. *British Journal of Social Work.* **29**: 269–284.

Barn R, Sinclair R and Ferdinand D (1997) *Acting on principle, an examination of race and ethnicity in social services provision for children and families.* BAAF, London.

Barter C (1999) *Protecting children from racism and racial abuse. A research review.* The NSPCC, London.

Batta I, Mc Culloch J and Smith N (1979) Colour as a variable in Childrens' Sections of Local Authority Social Services Departments. *New Community.* **7**: 78–84.

Begum N (1992). *Something to be proud of: The lives of Asian Disabled people and carers in Waltham Forest.* Race Relations Unit, London Borough of Waltham Forest.

Beresford B (1995) The needs of disabled children and their families. *Findings from social care research. No. 76.* Joseph Rowntree Foundation, York.

Berrington A (1996) Marriage patterns and inter-ethnic unions. In Coleman D and Salt J (eds) *Ethnicity in the 1991 census. Vol 1,* HMSO, London.

Bowlby J (1969) *Attachment and Loss, Vol I, Attachment.* Hogarth, London

Bowlby J (1973) *Attachment and Loss, Vol II, Separation: Anxiety and Anger.* Hogarth, London.

Bowlby J (1988) *A Secure Base: Clinical Applications of Attachment Theory.* Routledge, London.

The Bridge Child Care Consultancy Services (1991) *Sukina; An evaluation report of the circumstances leading to her death.* The Bridge, London.

Butt J and Box L (1998) *Family Centred. A study of the use of family centres by black families.* REU, London.

Butt J and Mirza K (1996) *Social care and black communities A review of recent research studies.* HMSO, London.

Carter H (1998) A joined-up solution to poverty. *Voluntary Voice No.129.* London Voluntary Services Council (LVSC), London.

Cashmore E (1984) *Dictionary of Race and Ethnic Relations.* Routledge, London.

CCETSW (1996) *Children, Spirituality and Religion. A Training Pack.* Central Council for Education and Training in Social Work, London.

Childline (1996) *Children and racism.* Childline, London.

Cross W E (1971) The Negro-to-Black Conversion Experience: Towards a Psychology of Black Liberation. *Black World. Volume 2.*

Donald J and Rattansi A (1992) *Race, Culture and Difference.* Sage, Bristol.

Dosanjh J S and Ghuman P A S (1997) Child Rearing Practices of Two Generations of Punjabi Parents. *Children and Society.* **11:** 29–43.

Dosanjh J S and Ghuman P A S (1998) Child Rearing Practices of Two Generations of Punjabi Parents: Development of Personality and Independence. *Children and Society.* **12:** 25–37.

Dutt R and Phillips M (1996) *Report of the National Commission of Inquiry into the Prevention of Child Abuse. Volume 2, Background Papers.* The Stationery Office, London.

Erikson E (1968) *Identity, Youth and Crisis.* Norton, New York.

Farmer E and Owen M (1995) *Child Protection Practice. Private Risks and Public Remedies.* HMSO, London.

Finkelhor D (1986) *A sourcebook on child sexual abuse.* Sage, London.

Gibbons J, Conroy S and Bell C (1995) *Operating the child protection system.* HMSO, London.

Grant L (1996) Parenting in Black Families. *The Parenting Forum Newsletter No.5.*

Haskey J (1997) Population Review (8). The ethnic minority and overseas-born population of Great Britain, Population Trends No. 88. Office of National Statistics, London.

Hoghhughi M and Speight A (1998) Good enough parenting for all children – a strategy for a healthier society. *Archives of Diseases in Childhood.* **78:** 293–300.

Hylton C (1997) *Family survival strategies.* Exploring Parenthood.

Jones T (1993) *Britain's Ethnic Minorities.* Policy Studies Institute, London.

Jones E and McCurdy K (1992) The links between child maltreatment and demographic characteristics of children. *Child Abuse and Neglect*, Vol 16.

Katz I (1996) *The Construction of Racial Identity in Children of Mixed Parentage. Mixed Metaphors.* Jessica Kingsley, London.

Klaus H and Kennel J (1976) *Maternal Infant Bonding.* Mosby, St Louis.

Kundnani H (1998) The sanction of last resort. *Voluntary Voice. No.129.* London Voluntary Services Council, London.

London Borough of Lambeth (1987) *Whose Child? The Report of the Panel of Inquiry into the Death of Tyra Henry 1987.* London Borough of Lambeth.

Macdonald S (1991) *All Equal Under the Act?* National Institute for Social Work, London.

MacPherson W (1999) *The Stephen Lawrence Inquiry. Report of an Inquiry.* The Stationery Office, London.

Milner D (1983) *Children and Race Ten Years On.* Ward Lock Educational, London.

Nazroo J Y (1997) *The Health of Britain's ethnic minorities. Findings from a national survey.* Policy Studies Institute, London.

NHS Executive (1998) *Sickle Cell Anaemia.* Department of Health, London.

Office for National Statistics (1996) *Social Focus on Ethnic Minorities.* HMSO, London.

Owen (1992) Ethnic Minorities in Great Britain: Settlement Patterns, 1999. Census Statistical Paper No 1. Centre for Research in Ethnic Relations, University of Warwick.

Owusu-Bempah J and Howitt D (1997) Socio-genealogical connectedness, attachment theory and child care practice. *Child and Family Social Work.* **2**: 199–207.

Owusu-Bempah K and Howitt D (1999) Even their soul is defective. *The Psychologist.* **12**: 3.

Phaure S (1991) *Who really cares? Models of voluntary sector community care and black communities.* London Voluntary Services Council, London.

Prohansky H and Gottleib N (1989) The development of place identity in the child. *Zero to Three.* **X**: 2, pp.18–25.

PSI (1997) *The Fourth National Survey of Ethnic Minorities in Britain, Diversity and Disadvantage.* PSI, London.

Reder P, Duncan S and Gray M (1993) *Beyond Blame, Child Abuse Tragedies Revisited.* Routledge, London.

Rowe J, Hundleby M and Garnett L (1989) *Child Care Now.* British Agency for Adoption and Fostering. Research Series 6.

Rutter M (1972) *Maternal Deprivation Reassessed.* Penguin, Harmondsworth.

Schaffer H and Emerson P (1964) The Development of Social Attachments in Infancy. *Monographs of Social Research in Child Development.* **29**: 94.

Sinclair I and Gibbs I (1998) *Children's Homes: A study in Diversity.* Wiley, Chichester.

Smaje C (1999) *Health, Race and Ethnicity. Making sense of the evidence.* Kings Fund Institute, London.

Social Exclusion Unit (1998) *Bringing Britain Together: A National Strategy for Neighbourhood Renewal.* The Stationary Office, London.

Social Services Inspectorate and Surrey County Council (1995) Unaccompanied Asylum-Seeking Children: A Training Pack. Department of Health, London.

Swanick M (1996) Child Rearing across Cultures. *Paediatric Nursing.* **8**(7): 13–17.

Thomas L (1995) *Multi-cultural Aspects of Attachment.* Internet.

Thoburn J, Lewis A and Shemmings D (1995) *Paternalism or partnership? Family involvement in the child protection process.* HMSO, London.

Tizard B and Phoenix A (1994) *Black, White or Mixed Race; Race and Racism in the Lives of Young People of Mixed Parentage.* Routledge, London.

Troyna B and Hatcher R (1992) *Racism in Childrens' Lives; A Study of Mainly White Primary Schools.* National Childrens Bureau/Routledge, New York.

# 3

## Assessing the needs of disabled children and their families

## Introduction

3.1　The Assessment Framework is designed to be inclusive of all children in need. Social Services Departments have a duty to ensure that every child is assessed in a way which recognises the child's individuality and particular needs. For many reasons, disabled children are more likely to come to the attention of health, education and social services and are far more likely to be assessed than other children. This guidance is therefore aimed at everyone involved in assessments, not just at those who have a specialist role with disabled children.

3.2　An assessment is a positive opportunity to identify and respond to the needs of children and families. It is most likely to be helpful to a child and family if it draws together multi-disciplinary expertise. Serious concerns have been raised about the quality of assessments of disabled children (Audit Commission, 1994; Department of Health, 1994; 1998a; 1998b; Morris, 1998b; Kagan et al,1998; Middleton,1999). The process of assessment and the likelihood of multiple assessment arrangements may compound the difficulties facing disabled children and their families and result in conflicting messages about the needs and the most effective types of intervention/or support. As stated in the Guidance (Department of Health et al, 2000, paragraph 1.42):

> … since discrimination of all kinds is an everyday reality in many children's lives, every effort must be made to ensure that agencies responses do not reflect or reinforce that experience and indeed, should counteract it.

3.3　In the past, disabled children have often been excluded from or marginalised within mainstream services, and many standard assessment frameworks and approaches have been developed with only non-disabled children in mind. The Children Act 1989 emphasises disabled children are 'children first' and the Assessment Framework is based on this principle of inclusion. However, recognising disabled children as children first does not imply denial of a child's particular needs: 'Ensuring equality of opportunity does not mean that all children are treated the same. It does mean understanding and working sensitively and knowledgeably with diversity...' (Department of Health et al, 2000, paragraph 1.43).

3.4　This practice guidance aims to assist those undertaking assessments of need, by enabling practitioners and managers to understand and work more sensitively with disabled children and their families. It is intended that the use of the Assessment Framework will mark a radical departure in assessment, moving from single agency service led assessments to assessments of the whole child by a co-ordinated group of professionals.

3.5    In preparation for this chapter Triangle consulted with disabled children through aMaze, a Brighton based project providing advice, information and support to assist parents to obtain the best for their disabled children. Quotes referenced as personal communication are from these groups and we are grateful for the children's consent to use their words.

## Disabled children and the Assessment Framework

3.6    The basic needs of disabled children are no different to those of any other child. The domains and dimensions of the Assessment Framework are relevant for all children. 'Professionals working with children need not and should not start from a different position when the children are disabled' (Middleton, 1999 p.92). While disabled children's basic needs are the same as all children's needs, impairments may create additional needs. Disabled children are also likely to face additional disabling barriers which inhibit or prevent their inclusion in society. The assessment of a disabled child must address the needs of the parent carers. Recognising the needs of parent carers is a core component in agreeing services which will promote the welfare of the disabled child. The main part of this chapter considers the needs and barriers in relation to each of the dimensions of the Assessment Framework.

3.7    The Assessment Framework is highly relevant for disabled children, for example the emphasis on responding to a child's individual needs; the expectation of children's involvement in the process; the commitment to working with parents and children; the emphasis on inter-agency working and the underlying ecological and empowerment models. A careful assessment that involves the child should be a helpful experience and result in real improvements in a child's life. Information from assessments can result in changes in the nature of service provision, especially if unmet need is recorded and used to inform children's services planning processes. Good quality assessments will also encourage active partnerships between mainstream and specialist services; working together to maximise disabled children's inclusion in family life, education and community services.

3.8    Depending on the definitions and methodology used, between 3% and 5% of children in the United Kingdom are classified as disabled (OPCS, 1986; Department of Health, 1998a). Different definitions of disability and a summary of the legislation are in Appendix 4.

3.9    Childhood disability arouses very strong feelings and touches on some of our most fundamental beliefs and assumptions. The cultural context in which assessments of disabled children take place is not a neutral one: disabled children and adults face major barriers to participating as equal members of our society. There are different ways of defining and understanding disability. Within the disabled people's movement, and within some services and some professional groups, there has been a move from an individual to a social model of disability. 'The individual model locates the 'problem' of disability within the individual and sees the causes as functional limitations or psycho-logical losses assumed to arise from disability'(Oliver, 1999, p.33).

3.10 This guidance is informed by an understanding of the 'social model' of disability, which uses the term disability not to refer to impairment (functional limitations) but rather to describe the effects of prejudice and discrimination: the social factors which create barriers, deny opportunities, and thereby dis-able people (Morris, 1998c; Oliver, 1999). Children's impairments can of course create genuine difficulties in their lives. However, many of the problems faced by disabled children are not caused by their conditions or impairments, but by societal values, service structures, or adult behaviour (Shakespeare and Watson, 1998):

> a major problem for disabled children is that they live in a society which views childhood impairment as deeply problematic (p.20).

3.11 Effective assessment of a disabled child must consider:

- the direct impact of a child's impairment;

- any disabling barriers that the child faces; and

- how to overcome such barriers.

## Disabled Children and assessment

3.12 Disabled children are far more likely than non-disabled children to be subject to multiple assessments by health, education and social services. There are several reasons for this:

- **There are more disabled children in groups already socially disadvantaged.** Whatever system is used to classify disability, there are twice the number of disabled children in social class 5 households as in social class 1 and there is a strong relationship between childhood disability and poverty/household income (Department of Health, 1998a; Dobson and Middleton,1999). The increased prevalence of certain impairments in some minority ethnic groups has also been linked to social disadvantage (Murphy et al, 1998).

- **Disabled children are more likely to have a number of experiences that may trigger assessment.** Disabled children face an increased risk of abuse (Westcott, 1993; Westcott and Cross, 1996; Westcott and Jones, 1999); and of school exclusion and social exclusion in its widest sense (Middleton, 1999). Disabled children are more likely to live away from home: to be accommodated on a short or long-term basis and/or to be in state-funded residential education.

- **Assessment has become the route to ordinary entitlements for many disabled children and their families.** Disabled children often have to be assessed to access the same basic provisions as non-disabled children, for example education, housing, play and leisure opportunities.

- **Assessment of special educational needs.** Many disabled children are assessed before they reach statutory school age because it is likely they will have special educational needs (SEN).

## Using assessments positively with disabled children and young people

3.13    When planning an assessment involving a disabled child it is important to:

- think about your own understanding of disability;

- take into account the child's experience and understanding of assessment;

- take into account the family's experience and understanding of assessment;

- be clear about the focus of an assessment;

- find out who else is currently involved with the child;

- gather information from existing assessments;

- access helpful information on specific childhood impairments.

Each of these areas will be addressed in turn.

3.14    **Think about your own understanding of disability.** Our perceptions of what it means to be disabled will affect our work. It is essential to actively explore our own attitudes and understanding, and to be aware of our own prejudices, fears and stereotypes about disability and about particular impairments. The inclusive approach of the Assessment Framework should be reflected in all areas of practice. Are disabled children made to feel welcome by your services? Is your building fully accessible? Do you employ disabled workers? Are your toys, books and resources suitable for all children? Are there positive images of disabled children around? Do you have a clear policy on anti-discriminatory practice? Are staff offered information, training and support on the inclusion of disabled children within the service? Is disability equality training offered to staff? Can facilities and approaches be adapted for the communication needs of disabled children, for example loop systems and/or use of signing for deaf children?

3.15    **Take into account the child's experience and understanding of assessment.** Disabled children are likely to have been assessed, often frequently, and often within a pathologising, deficit model where the child was tested against some concept of normality. For some disabled children, the very word assessment may have unhelpful connotations:

> *Its always about what's wrong with me ... they're only interested in the bits of me that don't work. They want to see what I can't do (11 year old disabled girl, personal communication).*

Disabled children and young people may not be used to active involvement in assessment processes. Children are entitled to an explanation of the assessment which is appropriate to their age and understanding. As far as is possible, the purpose should be agreed with the child as an assessment of their situation rather than of the child him or herself. This enables the child to become an essential part of the assessment team, contributing to information gathering and decision making, rather than being the passive focus of the exercise.

3.16    **Take into account the family's experience and understanding of assessment.** Families of disabled children will also have experienced many assessments. Some families describe dealing with service providers as the most difficult aspect of caring for their disabled children (Department of Health, 1998b, p.32). In one study, only 25% of parents of disabled children felt that assessment arrangements were well co-ordinated (Audit Commission, 1994). Assessments can undoubtedly be traumatic and difficult for some families:

> *I found assessment meetings a nightmare. I felt I was listening to people talk about somebody other than the child I lived with. After the first assessment at the child development centre I went home and cried for four days...* (Parent of disabled child, quoted in Murray and Penman, 1996).

3.17 Families require clear information about the focus of any assessment and about available services providing support. Parents should be clearly informed that their views and priorities are important and they should be encouraged to contribute to the process. The process should include recognition of the parent carers needs in bringing up their children.

3.18 Some families would like friends, advocates or relatives to support them during assessments and this should be facilitated. Experience with named persons in education indicates that discussions can be more positive and open when families who wish for support are accompanied by their own adviser or friend (Russell, 1999).

3.19 Parents of disabled children can be assigned multiple and sometimes contradictory roles by professionals. Twigg and Atkin (1993) describe the range of ways that professionals in social and health care systems conceptualise and respond to parents: they are perceived, simultaneously, as resources for the statutory services, co-workers and service recipients in their own right, while their children may or may not be also perceived as service recipients. This can create an ambiguous and confused relationship.

3.20 **Be clear about the focus of an assessment.** The Assessment Guidance states:

> However difficult the circumstances, the **purpose** of assessing the particular child and the family should always be kept in mind (paragraph 3.37).

3.21 Assessments should focus on the circumstances of the child and family and not just on an individual and whether a particular service is available. For disabled children in particular, there is a concern that assessments may be focused around assessing the child's problems, or assessing the child for specific services, rather than assessing the child's overall situation and needs. The most recent Department of Health inspection of services to disabled children found that 'There were very few needs-led assessments ... more frequently families were subject to a number of parallel assessments, often trawling through the same information but with a different service in mind' (Department of Health, 1998b, p.23).

3.22 Clarity of focus will also enable parents and children to contribute more effectively to an assessment. As an example, parents may perceive a broad assessment of a child's social integration that considers the possibility of using inclusive play and leisure facilities as an attempt to remove existing respite care arrangements. Clarity about the focus of the assessment is likely to diminish such anxieties.

3.23 In many cases practical help is most effective for a family with a disabled child, for example advice about benefits or the timely provision of aids and adaptations in the home. The needs of disabled children and their families for specialist disability equipment and assistive technology should be included in the assessment process. Equipment could range from a wheelchair and communication aid for the disabled child to special beds and lifting equipment to help parents or other carers. Assessment for equipment may need to involve several professionals on a multi-disciplinary basis and collaboration across agencies, particularly where different types of equipment have to be integrated. Where the relevant expertise is not available at local level, specialist centres such as communications aids centres may need to become involved. The views and wishes of the child and parents should be taken into account. A choice of equipment and the opportunity to try it out, for example by visiting a disabled living centre, should be offered as far as possible.

3.24 **Find out who else is involved currently with the child.** Assessment processes 'should be co-ordinated at all stages' (Department of Health, 1998b, p.57) and assessments of disabled children may be undertaken jointly with shared responsibility across agency boundaries (Department of Health et al, 2000).

3.25 Services for disabled children are often fragmented between different agencies. Different perspectives, values and professional languages can complicate working together across agency and discipline boundaries. Young disabled children often come sequentially to the attention of health, then education and then social services. Children who acquire their impairments may come suddenly into contact with all three agencies. Children with progressive conditions may have to switch between services and agencies as their needs change.

3.26 Within agencies, responsibilities for assessments of disabled children may also be located in different teams. For example, specialist social work teams for the deaf are often in either the disability or adult divisions, yet families obtain services from child care social workers or workers located in children with disabilities teams. Working across these boundaries can be facilitated by the development of a culture of co-working to harness all available expertise when assessing disabled children.

3.27 **Gather information from existing assessments.** Disabled children are likely to have already been assessed, and information already gathered should be accessed, having obtained consents as appropriate. Parents find it hard to tell their story again and again (Department of Health,1998b, p.22). Both children and family members often assume that agencies will share information with each other and may be surprised to find that they do not. Parents and children can be asked who they think has the most relevant knowledge – many have reported thinking the wrong professionals were consulted (Russell, 1999).

3.28 Integrated inter-agency assessment processes are in place in some areas and being developed in others (Russell, 1995; McConahie, 1997; Khan and Russell, 1999). Cross-agency key working can also enable effective information sharing (Mukherjee et al, 1999). Even where these mechanisms are not yet in place, information from other assessments should be available. For example, the *Code of Practice on the Identification and Assessment of Special Educational Needs* (Department for Education and Employment, 1994) requires local educational authorities to send a copy of the final statement of a child's special educational needs and accompanying advice to the social services department, whether or not social services have provided advice during the assessment process. It is good practice to seek parent's permission to send information to other agencies but where there are concerns about a child's safety local authorities may transfer information in the best interests of children without formal permission (see *Working Together to Safeguard Children* 1999, paragraphs 7.27 to 7.46).

3.29 **Access helpful information on specific childhood impairments.** It may be important to learn in general about the likely effects of an impairment or condition before meeting a child and his or her family. As a disabled teenager reported in Cross (1998) said:

> *I wish they knew more about disability, I mean, its sort of embarrassing to have to explain yourself (p.102).*

3.30 Learning about a child's condition does not mean becoming an expert. There are organisations of and for people with almost all impairments and conditions, and for parents. These are often good sources of accessible and up-to-date information[1]. It is important however to remember that every child experiences their condition differently. It will be important to understand the impact of an impairment on this child in this family as part of an assessment. Usually the best source of information will be the child and their family.

3.31 Given that disabled children will have had many experiences of having things done to them, it is important also to be careful about issues of consent and clarity of explanations. In particular 'pretend' choices should be avoided, where the child's consent is apparently sought but in reality the child has no choice: 'shall we take your coat off?', 'do you want this injection?', 'would you like to talk to me?'. Repeatedly being offered pretend choices can distort a child's experience and may contribute to disabled children's vulnerability to abuse. A good general rule is only to ask a question if you will go along with a refusal as well as acceptance.

## Domain: Child's Developmental Needs

3.32 All children need to be loved and valued for who they are, and all children have developmental needs. A disabled child's impairment(s) will affect a child's growth, development and physical or mental wellbeing to a greater or lesser degree. Some children will have many areas of development not affected by their impairments. Other impairments have more of a global impact. Like their non-disabled peers, the developmental needs of disabled children are formed by the interactions between their unique physiological and psychological characteristics, their social and emotional experiences within their families and their environment which includes prejudice and disabling barriers. Differentiating the impact of a child's impairment(s) from the impact of the child's experiences is important. Assessing concerns about a child's development requires particular clarity where a child is disabled.

3.33 'There must be a clear understanding of what a particular child is capable of achieving successfully at each stage of development, in order to ensure that he or she has the opportunity to achieve his or her full potential' (Department of Health et al, 2000,

---

1. Contact a Family provides help and advice for professional workers and families caring for disabled children through CONTACT LINE. Tel: 0171 383 3555. Fax: 0171 383 0259. The British Council of Disabled People is Britain's national umbrella organisation for groups controlled by disabled people. Tel: 01332 295551. Fax: 01332 295580. Minicom: 01332 295581.

paragraph 2.3). Assessment standards around developmental milestones should be used with great care. For example, early assessment of deaf children will enable access to language development, whether spoken or manual, as soon as possible following diagnosis.

3.34 A useful question in assessment is: 'Would I consider that option if the child were not disabled?'. Clear reasons are necessary if the answer is 'no' (Middleton, 1996).

---

 **Pointers for Practice**

**CHILD'S DEVELOPMENTAL NEEDS**

- Is the child loved and valued for who they are?

- Does the child's impairment directly affect his or her growth, development and physical or mental wellbeing?

- Are there disabling barriers which limit the child or otherwise hinder his or her development?

- What action can be taken to ensure that the child has maximum access to family, education and community life?

- What action can be taken to safeguard or support the child's development?

---

## Health

3.35 All children have the right to good health care. Disabled children have the same entitlements as other children to appropriate health care when ill, and to opportunities to maximise their wellbeing, including health and education. Additionally, disabled children's health, development and wellbeing, and sometimes their lives, may depend on specialist medical intervention. Health care in its wider sense can also reduce, prevent or sometimes cure functional impairments for some disabled children. Medical professionals are often the first to have contact with a disabled child and their family and can be major providers of information, advice and support throughout childhood. Child development centres can enable effective, holistic assessments of children by combining the skills of different professionals in one team.

3.36 The medical treatment of disabled children has led to some criticism. First, some children have been prescribed intrusive and quite vigorous treatments and therapies when the efficacy of the treatment is not known. These programmes may involve new, alternative or unorthodox approaches and concerns have been raised about the lack of safeguards: In the words of one critic, 'in the lives of disabled children ... anything goes as long as you call it therapeutic' (Oliver, 1999, p.107).

3.37 Second, therapy and treatment can imply deficiency (i.e. something wrong or bad that needs to be made better or put right), which can interfere with the development of a positive identity. Some disabled adults are now writing very critically about the unintended consequences of childhood medical experiences for the development of children's self-esteem (see French, 1993; 1996; Cross, 1998).

3.38 An unhelpful polarisation about the benefits of medical interventions has arisen where people argue in favour of the medical model or the social model without a case by case analysis of the likely benefits and possible disadvantages of specific treatments for individual children.

3.39 Most parents want what is best for their disabled child. However, there is not always consensus among parents, children and different professionals about the treatment or therapy that is best for a child. This is sometimes the case within orthodox medicine and there is less agreement about alternative or complementary medicine. Sometimes there is strong support from parents for a particular new treatment or therapy while psychologists and physicians may remain unconvinced of the efficacy of such innovations.

3.40 Consideration of the impact of both conventional and alternative treatments may thus be an important element of assessments involving disabled children. This does not only mean a clinical assessment of the efficacy of a particular treatment, but a holistic look at the impact of treatment or therapy on a child's life. Some therapies and treatments for disabled children can be disruptive, controversial and sometimes painful or distressing. The child may have to spend long periods of time in therapy, or away from home and therefore family. The longer term benefits of treatment will have to be considered alongside any short-term social and emotional costs to the child. Denying access to appropriate treatments and therapies could be neglectful or even abusive if the child's health or development is further impaired as a result.

3.41 A balanced approach to each child's individual needs is essential. The following guiding principle is useful: services should always meet a child's particular needs in ways that least disrupt the needs they have in common with all children, and treatments and therapies should be delivered in ways that least disrupt children's lives.

3.42 It is helpful to have ways assessing the validity and risk of new treatments. Some recent attempts have been made to give guidance on decisions about alternative treatments for particular conditions, specifically in relation to autism (Howlin, 1998) and cerebral palsy (McCarthy, 1999).

 **Pointers for Practice**

**DECISION-MAKING ABOUT TREATMENTS AND THERAPIES**

- How has the decision been made that this therapy is appropriate for this child?
- Can the decision wait until the child is of an age and understanding to be consulted?
- What can the child and family expect to gain or lose from the treatment?
- How long has the approach been used?
- What research is available on the treatment? What alternative interventions might be tried?
- Have the parents and/or the child had the opportunity to talk with others who have direct experience of the treatment?

## Issues of consent

3.43  In the light of the above, issues of consent are crucial. As noted in Volume 4 of the Guidance to the Children Act 1989 (Department of Health, 1991), disabled children's 'ability to give consent or refusal to any action, including assessment, examination or treatment is only limited by the general conditions relating to sufficient understanding which apply to other children under the Children Act' (p.14).

3.44  When children have learning or communication impairments it can be more difficult for professionals to address questions of consent, but it is arguably even more important that they do so. If a child resists or is distressed by a treatment or therapy, it is essential that treatment is reviewed urgently taking into account the child's perspective (for further discussion of consent to treatment and disabled children see Alderson, 1993; Chailey Heritage, 1997).

## Basic health care

3.45  Although disabled children generally have more contact with the medical world than other children, they may have more difficulty than non-disabled children in getting their basic healthcare needs met.

3.46  Disabled children can face barriers in accessing routine dental, optical, GP or hospital care. These barriers may include inaccessibility of buildings, inflexibility of systems, or attitudes of professionals. For example, one parent of a nine year old disabled boy commented:

> *I just can't take him to the surgery any more. He doesn't understand about waiting and he never sits down. The receptionists freeze if we walk in the door. Basically we wait until things are bad enough to call someone out or to go to the hospital* (Personal communication).

3.47  Discriminatory practice may need to be challenged: Disabled children may be given lower priority for scarce or expensive resources (Rutter and Seyman, 1999).

 **Pointers for Practice**

**HEALTH**

- Is the child getting access to basic health care?

- If not, what are the barriers?

- Is the child getting access to appropriate healthcare and treatment to maximise his or her quality of life?

- How does the child experience treatment or therapy?

- Are decisions about treatment and therapy being made on the basis of clear information?

- Has the child been consulted, and the child's views taken into account?

- If a child has been judged unable to give or withhold informed consent and is resisting treatment, is this being acknowledged and addressed?

- Does treatment or therapy disrupt the meeting of needs that the child shares with all children (for example, family life, friends, play)?

- Does treatment or therapy lead to unnecessary segregation or exclusion?

- If yes, can the treatment or therapy be managed differently, or are there other ways of helping the child?

---

## Education

3.48 Education is a key service for all children. Disabled children have the same entitlement to education as their peers. The *Framework for the Assessment of Children in Need and their Families* (Department of Health et al, 2000) emphasises the importance of taking 'account of a child's starting point and any special educational needs' (page 19).

3.49 Education legislation does not distinguish between disability and special educational needs. Under the Education Act 1996 a child is said to have special educational needs if (s)he has 'a learning difficulty which calls for special educational provisional to be made for him', and a child has a learning difficulty if:

> a. *he has a significantly greater difficulty in learning than the majority of children his age,*
>
> b. *he has a disability which either prevents or hinders him from making use of educational facilities of a kind generally provided for children of his age.*
>
> Education Act 1996

3.50 Thus not all children with special educational needs are disabled, and some disabled children do not have special educational needs. However, there is significant overlap between the two groups.

3.51 The *Code of Practice on the Identification and Assessment of Special Educational Needs* (1994) and the *Education Act 1996* set out the arrangements by which a child's special educational needs are identified, assessed and any appropriate provision made. Key principles of the Code of Practice are that:

- all children should have the greatest possible access to a broad and balanced education.

- all special educational needs must be addressed.

- children should be educated within mainstream schools wherever possible.

- active partnership between children, their parents, schools, LEAs and health and social services is essential in order to meet children's special educational needs.

3.52 Education policy and guidance thus 'confirm and amplify the key messages of the Children Act 1989', including the right of children to be heard in the assessment of their educational needs (Russell 1996, p.135).

3.53    Social services can play an important role in a Special Educational Needs assessment. They can ensure that parents have accurate information on assessment arrangements and local provision, and that the whole range of options is explained to the child and parents. They can provide an advocacy role for vulnerable children and families, including looked after children. They can facilitate integrated planning across agencies for the transition to adulthood.

---

→ **Pointers for Practice**

**EDUCATION**

- Are the child's educational needs being addressed?
- Are there barriers preventing the child accessing appropriate education?
- Is information being shared appropriately between agencies?
- Do parents and children have access to information about local provision?
- Are services from education co-ordinated and complementary to services from other agencies?

---

## Emotional and Behavioural Development

3.54    Disabled children and young people need to complete the same tasks of emotional development as all children: early attachments are just as important for disabled babies and children, and the development of relationships, self-confidence and sexuality are just as important for young disabled people. Disabled children and young people may need additional emotional support for all the same reasons as other children and young people: for example because of disruption of family relationships; loss; academic stress; serious illness; bullying or racism. Some Child and Adolescent Mental Health Services include staff, for example clinical psychologists, who have developed specific expertise in meeting the mental health needs of disabled children. Some counsellors have also developed expertise in this area (eg. see Brearley, 1997).

3.55    Some disabled children and young people thrive emotionally; others do not do well. The increased emphasis on listening to children should help practitioners better understand the emotional needs of disabled children at different stages in their lives.

3.56    Disabled children and young people may also need support with both the direct impact of their impairments and their experiences of prejudice and oppressive attitudes. It is important that such support is provided in ways that do not pathologise the child. Support from family, friends and professionals should not deny a child's experience of prejudice. Disabled young people and disabled adults may also be valuable sources of emotional support and understanding.

3.57    Disabled young people can face particular challenges during adolescence and the transition to adulthood (Hurst and Baldwin, 1994; Morris,1999c). Some of this is exacerbated by transitions between childhood and adult services. Sometimes different services have different ages at which this transition is deemed to take place.

*Rebecca's gap year before university was full of exciting opportunities, but Sam's gap year is remembered as the year everything ground to a halt* (Parent of disabled young adult, personal communication).

3.58 Recent publications clarify good practice in services involved in transition (Morris, 1999c; Department for Education & Employment, 1997). Choice, control, entitlement, consultation, involvement and inclusion are key themes.

3.59 Young disabled people from black and minority ethnic communities often face additional problems in their transition to adulthood. Services tend to be run by white people; insufficient account may be taken of the different meaning of adolescence in different cultures; young people who have spent time in residential education may have spent years with little or no contact with others from the same cultural background (Morris, 1999c).

3.60 At all ages, assessment of a child whose impairments have been caused or exacerbated by abuse raises particularly complex issues. The child's knowledge of the cause of their condition should be approached with extreme caution. Such knowledge can be truly unbearable for children, and they may genuinely not know about the abuse, even though they have apparently been told.

---

 **Pointers for Practice**

**EMOTIONAL AND BEHAVIOURAL DEVELOPMENT**

- Are there concerns about the child's emotional development?
- Can the child access sources of emotional support available to all children?
- If not, can disabling barriers be removed?
- Are appropriate supports available for transition to adulthood?
- Is there a way a disabled adult could help?

---

## Identity

3.61 The Assessment Framework refers to the 'strength of a positive sense of individuality'. Children's life chances will be affected by their sense of their own value and worth. Developing a positive sense of identity is an important task of childhood and adolescence, no less so for disabled children and young people. It has been noted that disabled children are often defined within a one dimensional identity that is largely 'degendered, asexual, culturally unspecific and classless' (Priestley, 1998, p.220). All aspects of a child's identity should be recognised, although different aspects will assume greater or lesser significance at different developmental stages.

3.62 Recognising disability as a positive identity is not easy in contemporary society. Disabled children growing up will receive negative messages about being disabled, and need a positive internal model of disabled identity to counteract negative stereotypes. Children can internalise the messages they receive about what it means to have an impairment. It can be difficult to develop a positive sense of identity as a young disabled person especially if services are entirely focused on changing the child through treatment, therapy, or other interventions. A child's impairment is an integral part of identity, not something separate or incidental. It is, of course, not the only aspect of their identity but should be considered throughout any assessment. It has been suggested that an early acceptance of a child's condition may be important for the development of a positive identity: 'children should make their journeys as themselves' (Middleton, 1999, p.129). We are also beginning to understand the importance of a family's perception of disability on a child's identity development. As an example, a differentiation needs to be made between deaf children in deaf families and deaf children of hearing parents. If deafness is considered normal, its impact will be different in comparison to a family where it may be viewed as a major disabling condition (Loosemore-Reppen, 1999).

3.63    There are strong parallels with issues for black children growing up in a racist society. There are also key differences. In terms of family context, black children usually have black families who can provide positive role models whereas disabled children usually have non-disabled parents. Many disabled children rarely meet disabled adults and may assume that they will somehow grow out of their impairments with age. This is a sensible assumption if one meets many disabled children and no disabled adults.

3.64    The cultural identity of disabled children should be recognised. Prejudice about race and disability can compound each other. There is evidence that families from minority ethnic groups caring for a severely disabled child are even more disadvantaged than white families in similar situations (Chamba et al, 1999).

3.65    Although it is not possible for any one professional to be fully knowledgeable about all childhood impairments and all cultural contexts, it is possible to demonstrate a willingness to learn about a child's individual needs and an openness to, and respect for, cultural differences. Of particular relevance when working with disabled children may be the cultural differences which exist within our society in relation to concepts such as dependence and independence. It is important to listen carefully to children and families' views about those differences.

3.66    In all cultures, disabled children may be perceived and treated as younger than their actual age. This is particularly so for learning disabled children and young people. Linked to this, the sexual identity of disabled children is often widely denied. Many disabled young people have very low expectations of relationships:

> I never dreamt that I'd get married and I certainly didn't think that I'd have children. It's something out of this world to me. Being disabled they made you feel as though you had no use in the world … It made me feel I wasn't whole, it made me feel sort of not clean enough to have children (Disabled woman in Humphries and Gordon, 1992, p.142).

3.67    There have been encouraging recent developments to ensure that disabled children have access to appropriate sex education (Adcock and Stanley, 1996; Scott and Kerr-Edwards, 1999).

**Pointers for Practice**

**IDENTITY**

- Is the child recognised as a girl or boy, as part of a family and community, with a definite cultural identity?

- Is the child recognised and treated in ways appropriate to his or her age and stage of development?

- Is the child's identity as a sexual being recognised in line with their age and understanding?

- Does the child have access to positive role models for all the different aspects of their identity?

- What messages is the child receiving about what it means to be disabled?

- Is the child loved and valued as they are, or are they learning that they need to change to be acceptable?

## Family and Social relationships

3.68 The great majority of disabled children grow up within their families and assessments should identify and support the strengths of families. All children need stable and affectionate relationships with their parents or carers, and all children need friends.

3.69 Relationships between families of disabled children and social services are often dominated by arrangements to separate children from their families through the provision of respite care (Morris,1998b). All parents and children need breaks from each other, but natural breaks (playing out, visiting friends, joining in organised activities, staying with relatives) may be unavailable to disabled children.

3.70 Defining the purpose of any service as respite can create a confusing situation. The child's experience of the service can become incidental since its defined purpose is to give the child's parents a break. A social model perspective is helpful in identifying children's real needs, which often require seeking ways to overcome disabling barriers that prevent them accessing the social and leisure opportunities available to their non-disabled peers.

3.71 All children need friends, and disabled children can face particular barriers in establishing and maintaining friendships:

> The disabled young people we interviewed more often led limited social lives ... The more severely disabled young people were least likely to have a wide circle of friends, close confidants or regular contact with their peers (Hurst and Baldwin, 1994, p.86).

3.72 Not all disabled children live at home. It is difficult to estimate how many live away from home: one figure commonly cited is that around 46,000 disabled children spend some or all of their time in residential establishments (Russell, 1994). Many of these children maintain strong family and social relationships but it is estimated that 'well over 4,000 disabled children and young people ... are living away from home, isolated from their families, and with little or no contact with people outside their schools, foster or residential homes and a circle of busy professionals' (Knight, 1998, p.58). An assessment should consider the requirement under the Children Act 1989 to appoint independent visitors for such isolated young people.

3.73  The continuation of relationships is important for all disabled children, particularly those who spend time away from their families, and have communication or learning impairments. If children do not read or write or use the telephone, other ways of staying in touch are necessary, for example photos, cassettes of voices, familiar sounds or music, videos, treasured belongings, objects of reference, life story books and things that smell like, taste like, or feel like home.

---

 **Pointers for Practice**

**FAMILY AND SOCIAL RELATIONSHIPS**

- Does the child belong within a family and community?

- Does the child have secure and stable attachments?

- Does the child have friends and are their friendships valued and supported?

- Should the child have the option of an independent visitor or other advocacy arrangement?

- Are the child's relationships within their family actively supported?

- Is the child's access to education, play or family life restricted by lack of support with their communication needs?

---

## Social Presentation

3.74  This dimension requires particular attention because disabled children and their families may experience pressure to deny or minimise or hide their impairments. 'The pressure to appear "normal" ... can give rise to enormous inefficiency and stress, yet many disabled people are well into adulthood before they abandon such attempts' (French,1993, p.46).

3.75  Denying one's situation and pretending to be 'normal' can be both exhausting and emotionally costly for children:

> ...having adults pretend that I could see more than I could, and having to acquiesce in the pretence, was a theme throughout my childhood ... as well as denying the reality of their disabilities, disabled children are frequently forced to deny painful feelings associated with their experiences because their parents and other adults simply cannot cope with them ... (French, 1993, p.69).

**SOCIAL PRESENTATION**

- Is the child supported to present themselves confidently, without denying or hiding impairments?
- Is the child helped to exercise choice about social presentation?

### Selfcare Skills

3.76 Selfcare and independence can be a major focus of services for disabled children. Independence is often thought to be something that disabled children and young people and indeed disabled adults desire above all else, yet 'the notion of independence can be taken too far, restricting the lives of disabled people rather than enriching them' (French, 1993, p.44).

3.77 Selfcare skills should be related to children's individual ability and desire to contribute to their care rather than be dictated by age. In assessments is important to listen carefully to children's views about undertaking their own care:

> Sammy was expected to spend around 90 minutes a day getting himself dressed and undressed, tasks which are very difficult because of his physical impairments. Sammy was given an opportunity to express his views about this routine and he communicated very strongly that he would rather spend that time reading or using his computer. As a result Sammy's routine was changed.

> Karen wanted to learn how to transfer from her wheelchair to a bath or bed. This proved a difficult skill that took some months for her to gain. She describes the impact of this one skill on her life as 'huge' and is very pleased she had the opportunity to learn how to do it.

3.78 Children's own priorities will vary and are likely to change over time. It is important also to be sensitive to fluctuations in children's abilities; tiredness, distress, illness or an unfamiliar environment can temporarily wipe out a skill.

 **Pointers for Practice**

**SELF-CARE SKILLS**

- Are the child's priorities in terms of self-care taken into account?
- Where the child receives personal care from others, is this undertaken respectfully?
- Are procedures explained to children before they occur?

## Domain: Parenting Capacity

Critically important to a child's health and development is the ability of parents or caregivers to ensure that the child's developmental needs are being appropriately and adequately responded to, and to adapt to his or her changing needs over time (Department of Health et al, 2000, paragraph 2.9).

3.79    The concept of reasonable parental care can be particularly challenging where a child is disabled. Some children need more parenting or more skilled parenting than others; some children need intensive parenting for much longer than others. Some children are parented in a far less supportive social context than others, and a consideration of the supports available to parents in responding to their child's needs is important (see next Domain). Some families have more than one disabled child which affects parenting capacity (Lawton, 1998).

3.80    Parenting a disabled child can be very demanding, both because of the child's impairments and because of the time and energy which have to be devoted to securing services to respond to the child's needs. When children have very complex needs and the demands on parents are heavy, there can be lower expectations of what constitutes reasonable parental care. Professionals may understandably think that parents do very well considering how little help they get and thus expectations of the standard of care which a disabled child should enjoy are lowered.

3.81    A clear value base at an individual and organisational level is essential for practitioners. The explicit commitment to equality of opportunity within the Assessment Framework should prove helpful in clarifying standards and expectations for disabled children.

 **Pointers for Practice**

**PARENTING CAPACITY**

• What supports are available to the help the family parent their disabled child?

• What is understood as constituting reasonable parental care given to this child?

• Are the standards for assessment of parenting capacity clear?

**Basic Care**

3.82    A disabled child's care needs might be more complex, take more time, or continue for more of their childhood, but basic care remains a right of all children.

3.83    A child's care needs can create barriers in their lives unless appropriate support is available; schools can be reluctant to give medication, playgroups may insist that children are out of nappies. Even services specifically for disabled children may exclude children with certain care needs, for example children who require tube feeding (see Townsley and Robinson, 1999). There may also be disagreements about whether basic care constitutes nursing or social care or is part of their education (and therefore which agency should pay). Identifying these barriers and finding ways to address them is an appropriate focus of assessment.

**Pointers for Practice**

**BASIC CARE**

- Are the child's basic care needs adequately responded to?

- If the child requires additional support, is this provided in ways that are both respectful of the child and sustainable in the long term?

- Is the child's access to education, play or family life restricted by lack of support with care needs?

## Emotional Warmth

3.84 'Ensuring the child's emotional needs are met and giving the child a sense of being specially valued' (Department of Health et al, 2000, page 21) is important for all children, but may be particularly crucial for disabled children who, given the societal context, are likely to receive negative messages about their personal value.

 **Pointers for Practice**

**EMOTIONAL WARMTH**

- Does the child experience warmth and affection from parents and/or caregivers?

- Does the child have secure, stable and affectionate relationships?

## Ensuring Safety

3.85 Disabled children are particularly vulnerable and face an increased risk of suffering abuse in many settings (Westcott and Jones, 1999). They ought to be over-represented in our child protection systems, yet research suggests that they may be significantly under-represented (Morris, 1998b; 1999a). The mistaken assumption that disability protects from abuse contributes to the vulnerability of disabled children.

3.86 The increased vulnerability of disabled children to abuse results from social attitudes and the special treatment of disabled children; for example, disabled children tend to be more isolated, to be more dependent, to have less control over their lives and their bodies, and may be less likely to be heard or believed. Disabled children are often in the care of many more adults than other children, they are more likely to spend time in institutional settings and the usual safeguards may not be in place (Morris, 1998b; Utting, 1997).

3.87 Possible indicators of abuse or significant harm may prove difficult to disentangle from the effects of a child's impairment. A multi-disciplinary approach is essential (Department of Health et al, 1999).

*A seven year old boy's constant masturbation was 'explained' by his autism and his attempts to touch adults sexually were initially attributed to his confusion about boundaries. Several years later his father was convicted of sexual assault of all three children in the family.*

*Severe self-injurious behaviour from a three year old was thought to be indicative of experience of violence at home, although there were no other indicators. As part of the assessment a second medical opinion was sought and the child was found to have a rare chromosomal disorder linked to self-injury and aggression.*

*Extensive bruising to the face, chest and arms of an eleven year old was said to result from falls during epileptic seizures. Medical advice was that the bruising was incompatible with falling and child protection procedures were initiated.*

3.88 Possible indicators may even be perceived as safeguards against abuse:

*Concerns were raised about the possible sexual abuse of a six year old girl with learning disabilities. School and residential staff felt she could not be abused because she resisted nappy changing with such violence.*

3.89 Assessments should consider the safety of the different settings in a child's life. There is some evidence that institutional care should be considered a risk factor in itself (Westcott, 1994). This information is relevant for many disabled children. For further discussion of safeguarding disabled children in institutions see Marchant and Cross (1993).

3.90 Munchausen syndrome by proxy is a very rare form of child abuse, and the possible links with childhood impairment are not yet fully understood. However, one possible consequence of repeatedly inducing illness in a child is long-term impairment. Preverbal children have been found to be at highest risk of induced illness (Schreiber and Libow, 1993) and anecdotal evidence suggests an increased incidence among disabled children (see Meadow, 1999; Precey, 1998).

3.91 There are welcome developments both in approaches for safety skills training specifically relevant for disabled children (Briggs, 1995; Kennedy, 1993a; 1993b; Lee et al, 1998; Marchant, 1998) and in approaches to making s47 enquiries regarding the possible abuse of children whose impairments affect their communication (Marchant and Page, 1993; 1997; Aldridge and Wood, 1998; 1999).

 **Pointers for Practice**

**ENSURING SAFETY**

- Are key adults in the child's life aware of the increased vulnerability of disabled children to being abused?

- Are standards for safeguards within services in place and regularly monitored?

- Can the child access the safety channels that exist for all children (e.g. helplines, complaints procedures, advocacy services)?

- If not, what alternative safeguards can be put in place?

- Have any concerns about possible significant harm been carefully considered and the subject of appropriate enquiries?

### Stimulation

3.92 All children need levels of stimulation appropriate to their stage of development and sensitive to their individual needs. Ideas, resources and support may be required to help parents of disabled children (especially children with multiple impairments or dual sensory impairments) to find appropriate ways to stimulate their child. On the other hand, parents may feel exceptional pressure to provide stimulation:

> *I found that you just do everything. Everything that came: "Yes, she'll do that, oh yes, we'll go to that, yes, we'll do that". I tried to carry on doing everything and then I couldn't manage really. But then it needed someone else to come in and say "Its alright, actually, you don't have to do all these things, and Alex will be perfectly fine if she doesn't do these things". I felt she needed so much input* (Parent of disabled girl in aMaze, 1997, p.26).

3.93 It may be an appropriate assessment task to help parents explore their child's need for stimulation and the connections with their own feelings about their child.

---

 **Pointers for Practice**

**STIMULATION**

- Is the child offered stimulation appropriate to their needs?

- Are parents able to access resources and ideas where needed?

- Does the child have access to recreation and leisure opportunities that provide stimulation?

---

### Guidance and Boundaries

3.94 All children need guidance and boundaries. Parenting disabled children can raise additional dilemmas when making decisions about reasonable risks. The dilemmas facing all parents may be magnified and assessments may encounter extremes of both over and under protection. Some parents of disabled children may need help to recognise that their child requires additional support or protection. Other parents need support and sometimes permission to let their disabled child take risks in their everyday lives.

3.95 Involving disabled adults in these discussions can be valuable:

> *Recently I was talking to a man with cerebral palsy and he was saying 'Let her do things, if people want to do things with her, let her do it. OK if she breaks an arm, she breaks an arm, but other children break arms you know. Just let her be a child* (Parent of disabled girl, in Beresford, 1994).

3.96 Disabled children are also more likely to be perceived as having challenging behaviour. The context of their lives may affect others' expectations: disabled young people can sometimes get away with less than others. It is useful to remind ourselves that most children and young people do not behave well all the time, they do not do what they are told immediately and without arguing, do not always go along with all adult suggestions, or do not always eat sensibly, get ready for school without protest or go to bed and get up again when asked.

3.97   That said, it seems that children with learning disabilities, autism, or language delay do face an increased risk of developing challenging behaviour. Physical and sensory impairments are also known to increase this likelihood. The increased likelihood of developing challenging behaviours is not necessarily a direct result of these impairments, but may be related to other factors.

3.98   Whatever the cause of a child's behaviour, and sometimes this is never absolutely clear, assessments must address the appropriateness of adult responses. Judgements about what constitutes reasonable control for disabled children can be particularly fraught. In assessments where there are issues around control of a child's behaviour, clear principles become essential (see also Mental Health Foundation (1997)).

---

 **Pointers for Practice**

**GUIDANCE AND BOUNDARIES**

- Is the child supported to take reasonable risks in everyday life?

- Are parents supported to enable children to take reasonable risks in everyday life?

- Are boundaries appropriate for the child's age and understanding?

- Do boundaries change over time as the child grows and develops?

- Is the child's welfare the paramount consideration?

- Are responses to a child's behaviour based on a consideration of what is in that child's best interests and what they would recognise themselves as being in their own interests, were they of the age and capacity to make such decisions themselves?

- Are restrictive measures adopted to deal with severe challenging behaviour only when there is no alternative?

- Are they used in the least detrimental manner and for the shortest possible time?

- Are measures of control part of a plan with long term strategies to meet the child's needs and encourage other behaviours?

- Have approaches been discussed by the parents, professionals and carers involved?

*Points 5 – 10 are adapted from Lyons (1994)*

---

## Stability

3.99   All children require stability in their lives. This does not mean absolute consistency. Most parents have breaks from their children, but these usually involve the child spending time in natural settings and with familiar people (friends, family). Disabled children may be unable to access these natural breaks and instead might be offered segregated services. Disabled children's patterns of care should offer stability appropriate to their age and understanding. They are more likely to face discontinuity in the short term (sleeping in several different places in one week) or in the long term (multiple changes of carers or of settings).

**Pointers for Practice**

**STABILITY**

- How many adults are involved in this child's life?
- Do they change frequently? Are there long term, secure attachment figures for the child?
- How many adults take care of this child?
- How many adults take intimate care of this child?
- How many different places or settings does this child sleep in?
- Is the care provided in different settings consistent?
- Is the care well planned and is the child properly prepared for breaks?

## Domain: Family And Environmental Factors

3.100 Parents' basic needs are the same whether or not their child is disabled. They need to feel supported, have breaks, feel valued and to have a family routine where they feel a sense of control. They benefit from professionals who respect them, and value and want the best for their child.

3.101 A wide range of factors can either help or hinder a family's functioning. The Assessment Framework acknowledges the inter-linking of different problems facing families. For families of disabled children this is a particularly important issue. Having a disabled child can impact on a family in many different ways. The direct effects of the child's impairment are likely to be compounded by disabling barriers facing both the child and the family.

3.102 These disabling barriers may be particularly daunting for families of disabled children who are otherwise at risk of social exclusion, for example because of their position in society, their family structure, their ethnic background, or their income.

3.103 Careful consideration of the supports available to parents in responding to their disabled child's needs is important. Many families make huge adjustments to respond to the needs of their children. Supports available to most parents are often less available to parents of disabled children. Baby-sitting and other informal supports may be much harder to find. Mainstream services (family centres, playgroups, nurseries) are often less accessible to families with disabled children. Living in a world that may relentlessly reject your child has an impact on families.

 **Pointers for Practice**

**FAMILY AND ENVIRONMENTAL FACTORS**

- What factors help or hinder this family's functioning?
- What disabling barriers face this family?

- What supports are available to this family in responding to the needs of their disabled child?

## Family History and Functioning

3.104 Exploration of the child's place within the family is important for disabled children as for all children. Relationships with parents and siblings require the same attention, as do parental strengths and difficulties. The birth of a child with some form of impairment, or the experience of a child acquiring an impairment is usually a significant life event, often perceived to disrupt family expectations for the future. The meaning that the impairment will hold for a family, and the family's response to such an event will depend on a range of factors. Exploring how a family has coped with other major life events may assist in placing responses in context.

3.105 Beresford (1994; 1995) emphasises the importance of defining parents as 'active agents' rather than 'passive recipients', thus acknowledging that they actively seek to manage the stresses and strains of caring for their disabled child. Services should seek to build on parents' strengths, and since parents cope in very different ways an approach sensitive to individual difference is necessary. There is good evidence that parents value highly assessments which take full account of their knowledge, understanding and aspirations for the future.

3.106 The siblings of disabled children have often been invisible to professional eyes. An assessment of a disabled child and their family should recognise the importance of siblings in each others' lives. Relationships between brothers and sisters should be valued and encouraged, including relationships where one or both children are disabled. It is essential to approach sibling relationships on an individual basis: it cannot be assumed that undertaking some caring responsibilities is harmful to siblings. The views of siblings about their relationships with each other may be an important part of the assessment.

 **Pointers for Practice**

**FAMILY HISTORY AND FUNCTIONING**

- How does this family generally cope with major life events?
- What place does the disabled child have within the family?
- What supports are available to this family?
- What are the effects on the siblings of the disabled child or children?
- Does any child undertake caring responsibilities for a disabled sibling which may be detrimental to his or her own development?

## Wider Family

3.107 The Assessment Framework stresses that 'Account must be taken of the diversity of family styles and structures, particularly who counts as a family and who is important to the child' (Department of Health et al, 2000, paragraph 2.15).

3.108 Like all children, disabled children will vary in the significance they attach to their wider family. Relationships with siblings, grandparents, other relatives, friends and neighbours may be crucial at different stages in a child's life. Wider family support is also important to parents: those who receive a lot of help from their extended family tend to report fewer unmet needs (Chamba et al, 1999). The assessment should therefore consider any potential within the wider family for increased support. There is some evidence that divorce is more likely in families with disabled children and so the assessment should include sensitive enquiries into ways in which an absent parent might be able to promote the child's welfare.

3.109 An important group of people for many disabled children are those who are paid to provide support to the child or who have been in the past, for example, teachers, carers, and outreach workers. A significant proportion of adults who provide family based care for disabled children have previously worked with disabled children in general or with the particular child they later care for.

3.110 Recent research found no evidence to substantiate the stereotype of extended supportive families among minority ethnic groups. Families' experiences, needs and circumstances vary across ethnic groups: Indian and Black African Caribbean families reported least support from their extended family, with levels of support lower than that found among the survey of white families. The most cited reason for lack of support was that no family members lived nearby (Chamba et al, 1999). In the same study, some Asian parents expressed the belief that they should bear full responsibility for their child and this prevented them from asking for help from their extended family.

 **Pointers for Practice**

**WIDER FAMILY**

- Who are the important people in this child's life?

- How are these relationships supported and preserved?

- Has the potential to offer support within the wider family (including any absent parents) been fully considered?

## Housing

The provision of appropriate housing can make an important contribution to meeting the health and developmental needs of children (Department of Health et al, 2000, paragraph 5.71).

3.111 Inadequate housing is a frequent barrier affecting families with children with a wide range of impairments, not just physical or mobility impairments. Housing that is unsuitable for a disabled child affects the whole family, by making it difficult or impossible for children to enjoy normal – even essential – childhood experiences.

3.112 For the disabled child, unsuitable housing can make moving around the house, playing, contributing to family life and learning to look after themselves much harder.

3.113 Issues raised in recent research include the general quality of housing; the amount of space; safety and access problems linked to location rather than to actual buildings (Beresford, 1994; Oldman and Beresford, 1998).

3.114 Oldsman and Beresford (1999) found that three out of four families reported one or more ways in which their housing was unsuitable; four out of ten reported than their housing was poor overall; and families with disabled children were more likely to live in rented housing on low incomes than families with non-disabled children. Families with disabled children often move for reasons associated with the child's impairment.

3.115 When houses are well adapted for a particular child, the family's life can be transformed:

> *If you can get your home right you can cope ... within 24 hours of being in this house ... she was a different child!* (Parent quoted in Oldman and Beresford, 1999).

3.116 Shortcomings in housing are likely to lead to demands for other services, for example short term breaks or help with lifting a child. This can both undermine a family's wish for independence and lead to a waste of limited public funds.

---

 **Pointers for Practice**

**HOUSING**

- Does the child's accommodation have basic amenities and facilities appropriate to the child's needs?

- Are advice and resources available to make the necessary adaptations?

---

## Employment

3.117 This dimension includes patterns of employment and impact of work on the child. We know that parents of disabled children face additional barriers to employment: very few mothers with a disabled child work outside the home – about 2% work full time compared with 23% of the general population of mothers with children (Lawton,1998). There are particularly low levels of employment among minority ethnic families with disabled children (Chamba et al, 1999) and among parents of more than one disabled child (Tozer, 1999).

3.118 Parents believe that employment has economic, social and psychological benefits for them and for their children, and assessments may helpfully explore barriers to employment with parents who wish to work.

3.119 This dimension also includes children's experience of work and its impact on them. It is important for disabled children to be aware of the world of work and if possible to see disabled adults in employment.

**Pointers for Practice**

**EMPLOYMENT**

- Are there barriers to employment if parents wish to work?

- Is accessible, adequate child care available?

- Do disabled young people have appropriate opportunities to experience work situations?

## Income

3.120 This dimension is about the sufficiency of income to meet the family's needs. Families are financially disadvantaged by having a disabled child, and it has been estimated that it costs on average three times more to bring up a severely disabled child than a non-disabled child (Dobson and Middleton, 1999). The same study found that younger disabled children are especially disadvantaged because the benefit system assumes lower costs for younger children, which is often not the case. Parents attempt to minimise the gap between their income and their spending by going into debt, spending less on themselves and other family members, and altering their lifestyles and aspirations.

3.121 Applying for financial help is a difficult process with an inherent tension: on the one hand parents are encouraged to promote their child's development but, on the other hand financial support and access to some services rests on levels of dependency. Applying for financial help can be emotionally difficult for parents:

> *I can't bear to do the DLA forms, its so painful to have to think about what she can't do and maybe will never do* (Parent of disabled girl, personal communication).

For these reasons the assessment should ensure that families are receiving the benefits to which they are entitled and are referred, if appropriate, to the Family Fund Trust.

3.122 Additionally, parents in a number of studies report difficulty in finding out about and claiming benefits (Kagan et al, 1998; Lawton, 1998; Dobson and Middleton, 1999). Minority ethnic group families were less likely to receive benefits and less likely to be awarded benefits at the higher rates than white families. Parents who understood English well had much higher levels of benefit take-up than those with little or no understanding of English (Chamba et al, 1999).

 **Pointers for Practice**

**INCOME**

- Are parents and young people clear about their financial entitlements?

- Is support available with applications for benefits?

- Is information about benefits accessible to all families?

- Have the cultural and linguistic backgrounds of the families been fully taken into account?

- Are working parents of disabled children aware of their entitlement to benefits?

## Family's Social Integration

3.123 Assessments should consider the wider social context and a family's social integration or isolation. Families of disabled children can face barriers to social integration, which may be physical, financial or attitudinal.

3.124 Relationships with other families are an important part of life. Disabled children and their families may face barriers preventing them from taking part in social events or cultural or religious celebrations or holidays. Providing the appropriate form of support may enable disabled children to join with their families in such events, and on a more day to day basis may enable children to go to their local playgroup, park, school, church, swimming pool or youth club, or to visit friends of the family or relatives. Supporting the social integration of disabled children often facilitates the integration of their parents, who gain opportunities to meet local parents at the school gate, local members of their religious community, workers in local services and so on. Many families welcome introductions to support groups as a means of reducing social isolation, and gaining useful information and valued support.

 **Pointers for Practice**

**FAMILY'S SOCIAL INTEGRATION**

- Does the family face barriers to their social integration?

- Can supports be provided to facilitate the child and family's integration?

## Community Resources

3.125 This dimension includes the availability and accessibility of local resources to children and families. Assessments should consider barriers to the disabled child's use of community resources:

> Disabled children have the human right to take part in play and leisure activities and to freely express themselves in cultural and artistic ways. They have the right to equal access to cultural, artistic, recreational and leisure activities (Morris, 1998c, p.20).

Assessments should therefore focus on disabled children's needs for support to enable them to access leisure, recreation and play activities. The Disability Discrimination Act 1995 should result in a wide range of resources being more accessible to disabled children.

3.126 The Disability Discrimination Act 1995 has put those who provide services to the public (eg shops, banks, leisure facilities, as well as health and social services themselves) under new duties to make their services more accessible to disabled people. Since 1996, it is has generally been illegal for service providers to discriminate against disabled people by refusing to provide them with a service on the same terms as are available to the public generally. Since October 1999 service providers have been required to take "reasonable steps" to make their services accessible to disabled people who would otherwise find them impossible or unreasonably difficult to access. (Further information about the Disability Discrimination Act's requirements of service providers, including the Code of Practice on access to goods and services, is available on the Government's disability website http://www.disability.gov.uk). These duties should make it easier for disabled children to access mainstream services: they do not, however, remove the need for social services to continue to provide special support where services would otherwise be inaccessible.

3.127 Disabled adults are also a potentially valuable community resource for disabled children and their families. The disabled people's movement is paying increasing attention to children's issues (see Cross, 1998; Morris, 1998c; Shakespeare and Watson, 1998).

> *I learn more from them (disabled adults) than I can learn from anybody, about what their childhoods were like…* (Parent quoted in Beresford, 1994).

---

 **Pointers for Practice**

**COMMUNITY RESOURCES**

- Is the child linked into their community resources?
- Can they and do they make use of community resources?
- What steps are being taken to overcome barriers to inclusion?

---

### Involving children in the assessment process

3.128 Involving disabled children and young people in assessments has a value in its own right, quite apart from the improved quality of assessment that is likely to result in. It demonstrates to children and others a respect and valuing of the child as a person.

3.129 Workers may face a number of barriers when involving disabled children in assessments. This final section is designed to address some of these in very practical ways.

3.130 **Others may not expect this to happen.** Be clear from the start that you want to involve children in the assessment. Others may not expect it to happen: parents, children and other workers may be surprised as the child may not previously have been consulted. Children may also be unused to participation. Actively involving children in decision making may be threatening for parents – many families do not routinely involve children, disabled or not, in family decisions. Prepare parents and attend to their concerns.

3.131 **Workers may not feel confident about their own skills.** Social workers who are generally good at communicating with children are likely also to be good at communicating with disabled children, but may need encouragement and support to adapt their skills and try out new approaches. General listening and communications skills are usually more useful than attempting to become competent in a wide range of communication methods.

3.132 **Develop a broad and flexible definition of communication.** Involving children with communication impairments in meaningful ways requires us to broaden our definition of communication and to be willing to try new approaches (Marchant and Martyn, 1999). Individualised, responsive ways of working are essential.

3.133 We often act as if speaking is the only valid way to communicate and yet we know that this is rarely the case for any child. Total communication means tuning in on all channels, attending for example: to speech; sign; symbols; body language; facial expression; gesture; behaviour; art; photographs; objects of reference; games; drawing and playing.

3.134 Recent work suggests innovative ways to engage with and consult disabled children (Beresford, 1997; Sanderson et al, 1997; Ward, 1997; Beecher, 1998; Morris, 1998d; Russell, 1998; Griffiths et al, 1999; Kirkbride, 1999; Marchant et al, 1999; Morris, 1999b; Prewett, 1999). Being alongside children – endeavouring to observe their world from their point of view – can be a potent assessment tool.

3.135 **Standard assessment approaches may not work.** One parent arrived at her son's annual review with a blank, chewed copy of the form she had been sent to record his views. She wrote to social services:

> *I have no problem with you consulting my child. In fact I would like to know how to do so myself. But sending him this questionnaire is just bizarre. I showed him the form and he tried to eat it* (Parent of 13 year old boy with severe learning disabilities and autism, personal communication).

3.136 **Involve others who can support communication with the child.** Find out about the child's communication from the child and from others who know the child well. If possible, ask the child whom to approach. Sometimes communication with a child will need the help of a third party. Independent interpreters are often not available for children with complex needs, whose communication methods may be very idiosyncratic. The ideal is someone who knows the child well, is trusted by the child and is as neutral as possible about the assessment.

> *Paul is 9 and communicates using eye pointing on a personalised communication board of words and symbols. He spends his time at residential school and in foster care. His social worker finds out who can communicate well with him, and offers Paul a choice of three people to help her involve him **in the assessment process.***

This gives Paul control within safe boundaries.

3.137 **If parents or others are to be directly involved negotiate clear ground rules at the start.** Sometimes establishing direct communication with a child is far easier than anticipated:

> *Janice is 13 and communicates with gestures, signs and some words although her speech is difficult to understand. Her social worker spent time with her at home and at school. She and Janice became more confident in each others' presence and after two visits were able to communicate directly with each other without any help.*

3.138 **Be responsive and flexible.** The following are suggestions for practitioners about how to be responsive to the needs and views of each child:

- make approaches to the young people responsive and individualised;

- where appropriate, encourage or allow young people to do other things at the same time as communicating (playing, drawing, walking, eating or drinking);

- take interesting things in a bag or folder that you are willing to let the child look through;

- have lots of different ideas ready, and be prepared to abandon them all;

- be non-directive, reflect back to young people what they have said, ask open questions;

- acknowledge if things aren't going well, say if you don't understand, be willing to go back to the beginning and start again;

- listen carefully to everything being communicated, especially where there is a discrepancy between verbal and non-verbal messages;

- don't make assumptions, keep an open mind, check back;

- let it take time, go at the young person's pace, be willing to wait, be willing to take a break, to stop and try again.

## Conclusion

3.139 It is an exciting time to be involved in assessment work with disabled children: knowledge and resources are developing rapidly and our understanding of what it means to be disabled are being challenged. Assessment represents a powerful force for change.

3.140 The basic needs of disabled children and their families are no different to those of any other child and family. Those involved in assessments must bear in mind the context, and be both aware of and prepared to challenge disabling barriers in a child's life. Inclusive practice has benefits beyond the effects for individual children and families. Getting assessments right for children with the most complex needs will improve practice with all children.

> *Everybody's got something different about them, and somethings are just more different than others. But we're all – I don't know – different in different ways* (Disabled girl of 12, quoted in Cavet, 1999, p.91).

# APPENDIX 4
## Definitions of Disability and Key Legislation

### Children Act 1989

In section 17 of the Children Act 1989 a child is defined as in need if:

*a) he is unlikely to achieve or maintain, or to have the opportunity of achieving or maintaining a reasonable standard of health or development without the provision for him of services by a local under this [Part] of the Act.*

*b) his health or development is likely to be significantly impaired, or further impaired, without the provision for him of such services or*

*c) he is disabled.*

> *'Development' means physical, intellectual, emotional, social or behavioural development and*

> *'health' means physical or mental health.*

The Children Act mirrors the National Assistance 1948 definition of disability, which states that:

> *A child is disabled if he is blind, deaf or dumb or suffers from mental disorder of any kind or is substantially and permanently handicapped by illness, injury or congenital deformity or such other disability as may be prescribed.*

### World Health Organisation

There have been ongoing debates in the United Kingdom and elsewhere about definitions of disability. The World Health Organisation defines disability under four key headings, namely:

a) A disorder: a medically definable condition such as spina bifida;

b) An impairment: any loss or abnormality of physiological, psychological or anatomical function or structure (eg paraplegia);

c) A disability: any restriction or loss arising from an impairment, of the ability to carry out an activity in a way or within the range of that would be considered normal for a person of a similar age (eg the ability to walk);

d) A handicap: the impact of the impairment or disability upon the individual's pursuit or achievement of the goals which he/she wishes or expects, or which may be desired or expected by him/her or by society (eg. The inability to undertake particular forms of employment or to live independently).

The World Health Organisation definitions are currently under review.

## Disability Discrimination Act 1995

*The Disability Discrimination Act* (1995) defines a disabled person as someone who has:

> *A physical or mental impairment which has a substantial and long-term adverse effects on his ability to carry out normal day-to-day activities.*

*The Disability Rights Task Force* (1999) identified a number of weaknesses within the DDA definition of disability and its interpretation. It has therefore recommended that the Disability Rights Commission, when established, should further review and consult on the question of definitions of disability.

## Disabled People's International

Organisations of disabled people have become increasingly concerned at the impact of negative definitions of disability, arguing that the social model of disability should be adopted in place of a model based upon deficits. The British Council of Disabled People has adopted Disabled People's International's definitions of disability, namely that:

> Disability is the loss or limitation of the ability to take part in the normal life of the community on an equal level with others, due to physical and social barriers.

## Education Act 1996

The majority of (although not all) children with disabilities will also have special educational needs. Section 316 of the Education Act 1996 defines disability in the context of special educational needs as follows:

Section 312(1)

> *A child has 'special educational needs' for the purposes of this Act fi he has a learning difficulty which calls for special education provision to be made for him.*

A child may be defined as having a learning difficulty calling for special educational provision if:

> *He has a disability which either prevents or hinders him from making use of educational facilities of a kind generally provided for children of his age in schools within the area of the local education authority.*

Any assessment of a child with a disability should not only have regard to definitions of disability under the Children Act 1989 and the Disability Discrimination Act 1995 (with reference to access to goods and services) but also consider the implications of the child's disability for his educational development and progression.

## Some Key Legislation Relevant to the Assessment of Disabled Children

The following legislation is of particular relevance to the assessment of disabled children:

### The Carers (Representation and Services) Act 1995

The Carers' Act makes provision for parents and carers (including young carers) to request independent assessments of their needs, when the child or adult cared for is undergoing as assessment under Section 47 of the NHS and Community Care Act 1990, the Children Act 1989 or the Chronically Sick and Disabled Persons Act 1970.

### The Children Act 1989

The Children Act 1989 brings together most public and private law relating to children in England and Wales. Section 17 clarifies the position of children with disabilities as *children in need* and therefore eligible for a range of services and support from the local authority. Schedule 2 permits a local authority to assess a child's needs at the same time as other assessments under different legislation (for example under the Education Act 1996). *The Children Act 1989 Guidance and Regulations, Volume 6: Children with Disabilities* gives further information.

### The Chronically Sick and Disabled Persons Act 1970 (CSDPA)

Section 2 of the CSDPA requires authorities to make arrangements for the provision of a number of services (such as practical assistance in the home or access to leisure and recreational facilities) if they are satisfied that it is necessary to do so in order to meet the disabled person's needs.

### The Community Care (Direct Payments) Act 1996

The Community Care (Direct Payments) Act is designed to enable local authorities to make direct payments to service users in order to purchase their own communication care.

### The Carers and Disabled Children Bill

The Carers and Disabled Children Bill proposes, subject to Royal Assent, to extend direct payments to disabled 16 and 17 year olds and to parents of disabled children.

### The Disability Discrimination Act 1995 (DDA)

From December 1996 it has been unlawful for service providers to treat disabled people less favourably for a reason related to their disability. Since October 1999, service providers (including health and social services) have been required to make 'reasonable adjustments' or provide an alternative method of service when practices, policies or procedures to make it impossible or unreasonably difficult for a disabled child or adult to use the service in question. The *Code of Practice on Rights of Access: Goods, Facilities, Services and Premises* (1999) sets out the relevant duties for local authorities in the provision of services. A Disability Rights Commission was established in April 2000.

**The Disabled Persons (Services, Consultation and Representation) Act 1986 (DPA)**

This Act supplements the provisions of the CSDPA 1970. Section 4 requires authorities to assess need for services under Section 2 of the CSDPA. Sections 5 and 6 require authorities to identify disabled school leavers and assess their need for social services. Section 9 amends the Section 1 of the CSDPA with regard to provision of information.

**The Education Act 1996**

The Education Act 1996 specifies the procedures to be followed by Local Education Authorities (LEAs) with regard to the identification and assessment of children with special educational needs and any special educational provision arising from assessment. The Act is accompanied by a Code of Practice (*Code of Practice on the Identification and Assessment of Special Education Needs* (1994)) which clarifies the contributions of social services departments and child health services, as well as schools and the LEA, in assessing special educational needs.

**The Local Government and Housing Act 1999**

Under section 114, local housing authorities are able to give *disabled facilities grants* to disabled people (including disabled children) to help with the costs of adaptations to enable them to live as independently as possible in their own homes.

**The NHS and Community Care Act 1990**

The NHS and Community Care Act 1990 requires social services departments to assess the needs of persons who may require community care services and, if appropriate, to provide 'care packages' in the light of the users' circumstances. The Act relates to adults and not to children, but is relevant to assessment for transition plans.

# References – Chapter 3

ABCD (1993) *Abuse and Disabled Children: Training and Resource Pack for Trainers in Child Protection and Disability.* The NSPCC, London.

Adcock K and Stanley G (1996) *Sexual Health, Education and Children and Young People with Learning Disabilities.* BILD, Kidderminster.

Alderson P (1993) *Children's Consent to Surgery.* Open University Press, Buckingham.

Aldridge M and Wood J (1998) *Interviewing Children: A Guide for Childcare and Forensic Practitioners.* Wiley, Chichester.

Aldridge M and Wood J (1999) Interviewing child witnesses with disabilities: A survey of police officers in England and Wales. *The Police Journal.* January 1999. pp.33–42.

The aMaze Project (1997) *Through the Maze: An information handbook for parents of children with special needs.* aMaze, Brighton.

Argent H and Kerrane A (1997) *Taking Extra Care: Respite, Shared and Permanent Care for Children with Disabilities.* BAAF, London.

Audit Commission (1994) *Seen but not Heard: Co-ordinating Community Child Health and Social Services.* HMSO, London.

Bakheit M, Chamba R, Griffiths J, Lee D and Marchant R (1999) *Recommendations for minimum standards of health care in children with cerebral palsy.* Bell-Pottinger Health Care.

Beecher W (1998) *Having a Say! Disabled Children and Effective Partnership: Section 2 – Practice Initiatives and Selected Annotated References.* Council for Disabled Children, London.

Beresford B (1994) *Positively Parents: Caring for a Severely Disabled Child.* Social Policy Research Unit, York.

Beresford B (1995) *Expert Opinions: A National Survey of Parents Caring for a Severely Disabled Child.* Policy Press, Bristol.

Beresford B (1997) *Personal Accounts: Involving Disabled Children in Research.* Social Policy Research Unit, York.

Brearley G (1997) *Counselling Children with Special Needs.* Blackwell Science, Oxford.

Briggs F (1995) *Developing Personal Safety Skills in Children with Disabilities.* Jessica Kingsley, London.

Cavet J (1998) *People Don't Understand: Children, Young People and their Families living with a Hidden Disability.* National Children's Bureau, London.

Chamba R, Ahmad W, Hirst M, Lawton D and Beresford B (1999) *On the Edge: Minority Ethnic Families Caring for a Severely Disabled Child.* Policy Press, London.

Chailey Heritage (1997) *Guidelines for Good Practice in Consent to Examination or Treatment.* Chailey Heritage, Sussex.

*Children Act 1989* (1989) HMSO, London.

Cross M (1998) *Proud Child, Safer Child: A Handbook for Parents and Carers of Disabled Children.* Women's Press, London.

Department for Education and Employment (1994) *The Code of Practice on the Identification and Assessment of Special Educational Needs.* HMSO, London.

Department for Education and Employment (1997) *Making Connections: A Guide for agencies helping young people with disabilities make the transition from school to adulthood.* The Stationery Office, London.

Department of Health (1991) *The Children Act 1989 Guidance and Regulations: Volume 6: Children with Disabilities.* HMSO, London.

Department of Health (1994) *Services to Disabled Children and their Families: Report of the National Inspection.* Department of Health, London.

Department of Health (1998a) *Disabled Children: Directions for their Future Care.* Department of Health, London.

Department of Health (1998b) *Removing Barriers for Disabled Children: Inspection of Services to Disabled Children and their Families.* Department of Health, London.

Department of Health (1999) *Stepping away from the edge.* Department of Health, London.

Department of Health, Department for Education and Employment and The Home Office (2000) *Framework for the Assessment of Children in Need and their Families.* The Stationery Office, London.

Department of Health, Home Office, Department for Education and Employment (1999) *Working Together to Safeguard Children: A guide to inter-agency working to safeguard and promote the welfare of children.* The Stationery Office, London.

Department of Health and the Welsh Office (1997) *People Like Us. The Report of the Review of the Safeguards for Children Living Away from Home.* The Stationery Office, London.

*Disability Discrimination Act 1995* (1995) The Stationery Office, London.

Dobson B and Middleton S (1999) *Paying to Care: The Cost of Childhood Disability.* York Publishing Services, York.

*Education Act 1996* (1996) The Stationery Office, London.

French S (1993) *Can you see the Rainbow? The roots of denial.* In Finkelstein V (ed) *Disabling Barriers, Enabling Environments.* Sage, London.

French S (1996) *Out of Sight, Out of Mind: The experience and effects of a "special" residential school.* In Morris J (ed) *Encounters with Strangers: Feminism and Disability.* Women's Press, London.

Griffiths J, Cunningham G and Dick S (1999) *Onwards and Upwards: Involving Disabled Children and Young People in Decision Making.* Children in Scotland, Edinburgh.

Howlin P (1998) *Children with Autism and Asperger Syndrome: A Guide for Practioners and Carers.* Wiley, Chichester.

Humphries S and Gordon P (1992) *Out of Sight: The experience of Disability 1900–1950.* Northcote House, London.

Hurst M and Baldwin S (1994) *Unequal Opportunities: Growing up Disabled.* HMSO, London.

Joseph Rowntree Foundation (1999) *Supporting Disabled Children and their Families: summary of research findings.* Joseph Rowntree Foundation, York.

Kagan C, Lewis S and Heaton P (1998) *Caring to Work: Accounts of Working Parents of Disabled Children.* Family Policy Studies Centre, London.

Khan J and Russell P (1999) *Quality Protects: First analysis of management action plans with reference to disabled children and families.* Council for Disabled Children, London.

Kennedy M (1993a) *You Choose.* National Deaf Children's Society, London.

Kennedy M (1993b) *Safety and prevention programmes.* In *ABCD Reader.* pp.43–38. The NSPCC, London.

Kirkbride L (1999) *I'll go First: The Planning and Review Toolkit for use with Children with Disabilities.* Children's Society, London.

Knight A (1998) *Valued or Forgotten? Independent Vistors and Disabled Young People.* National Children's Bureau, London.

Lawton D (1998) *Complex Numbers: Families with more than one disabled child.* Social Policy Research Unit, York.

Lee D, McGee A and Ungar S (1998) Issues in the development of a computer based safety programme for children with severe learning difficulties. *Child Abuse Review.* 7: 343–354.

Loosemore-Reppen G (1999) *Personal Communication.*

Lyons C (1994) *Legal Issues arising from the care and control of Children with Learning Disabilities who also present Severely Challenging Behaviour.* Mental Health Foundation, London.

McConahie H (1997) Organisation of child disability services. *Child: care, health and development.* 23: 1, pp.3–9.

McCarthy G (1999) *Additional therapies for children with cerebral palsy.* Scope School for Parents Conference.

Marchant R (1998) *Letting it Take Time.* In Ward, L. (ed) *Innovations in Advocacy and Empowerment for People with Intellectual Disabilities.* Liseux Hall, Lancashire.

Marchant R and Cross M (1993) *Places of Safety: Institutions, disabled children and abuse.* In *ABCD Reader.* The NSPCC, London.

Marchant R and Page M (1993) *Bridging the Gap: Child Protection work with Children with Multiple Disabilities.* The NSPCC, London.

Marchant R and Page M (1997) *The Memorandum and Disabled Children.* In Westcott J and Jones J (1997) *Perspectives on the Memorandum: Policy, Practice and Research.* Arena, Aldershot.

Marchant R, Jones M, Giles A and Julyan A (1999) *Listening on all Channels: Consulting with Disabled Children.* Triangle, Brighton.

Marchant R and Martyn M (1999) *Make it Happen: Communication Handbook.* Triangle, Brighton.

Meadow R (1999) Mothering to death. *Archives of Diseases in Childhood.* 80: 359–362.

Mental Health Foundation (1997) *Don't Forget Us: children with learning disabilities and severe challenging behaviour.* Mental Health Foundation, London.

Middleton L (1996) *Making a Difference: Social Work with Disabled Children*. Venture Press, Birmingham.

Middleton L (1999) *Disabled Children: Challenging Social Exclusion*. Blackwell, Oxford.

Morris J (1995) *Gone Missing? A Research and Policy Review of Disabled Children Living away from their Families*. The Who Cares? Trust, London.

Morris J (1998a) *Still Missing? Vol 1: The Experiences of Disabled Children living away from their Families*. The Who Cares? Trust, London.

Morris J (1998b) *Still Missing? Vol 2: Disabled Children and the Children Act*. The Who Cares? Trust, London.

Morris J (1998c) *Accessing Human Rights: Disabled Children and the Children Act*. Barnardo's, London.

Morris J (1998d) *Don't Leave us Out: Involving Children and Young People with Communication Impairments*. York Publishing Services, York.

Morris J (1999a) Disabled children, child protection systems and the Children Act 1989. *Child Abuse Review*. **8**:91–108.

Morris J (1999b) *Space for Us: Finding out what Disabled Children and Young People think about their Placements*. Newham Social Services Department, London.

Morris J (1999c) *Move On Up: Supporting Young Disabled People in the Transition to Adulthood*. Barnardo's, London.

Mukherjee S, Beresford B and Sloper P (1999) *Unlocking keyworking: An analysis and evaluation of keyworker services for families with disabled children*. The Policy Press/Community Care, London.

Murphy C C, Boyle C, Schendel D, Decoufle P and Yeargin-Allsop M (1998) Epidemiology of mental retardation in children. *Mental Retardation and Developmental Disabilities Research Reviews*. **4**: 6–13.

Murray P and Penman J (1996) *Let Our Children Be: A Collection of Stories*. Parents with Attitude, Sheffield.

Oldman C and Beresford B (1998) *Homes Unfit for Children: Housing Disabled Children and their Families*. Policy Press, Bristol.

OPCS (1986) *Surveys of Disability in Great Britain. Reports 1–6*. HMSO, London.

Oliver M (1999) *Understanding Disability: From Theory to Practice*. MacMillan, London.

Oswin M (1992) *They Keep Going Away: A critical study of short term residential care services for children with learning difficulties*. Kings Fund Centre, London.

Precey G (1998) Assessment issues in working with mothers who induce illness in their children. *Child and Family Social Work, Vol 3*. Blackwell Science Ltd, London.

Prewett E (1999) *Short Term Break, Long Term Benefit: Family based short term care for disabled children and adults*. University of Sheffield and Joseph Rowntree Foundation, Bristol.

Priestley M (1998) Childhood disability and disabled childhoods: agendas for research. *Childhood*. 5(2): 207–23.

Russell P (1994) *The Children Act 1989: Children and Young People with Learning Difficulties – Some Opportunities and Challenges.* Council for Disabled Children, London.

Russell P (1995) *Positive Choices: Services for Disabled Children Living Away from Home.* Council for Disabled Children, London.

Russell P (1996) *Listening to Children with special educational needs.* In Davie R and Galloway D (eds) *Listening to Children in Education.* David Fulton, London.

Russell P (1998) *Having a Say: Disabled Children and Effective Partnership in Decision Making: Section 1 The Report.* Council for Disabled Children, London.

Russell P (1999) *Personal communication.*

Rutter S and Seyman S (1999) *'He'll never join the army'. A report on a survey into attitudes to people with Down's Syndrome amongst medical professionals.* Down's Syndrome Association, London.

Robinson C and Stalker K (eds) (1998) *Growing up with Disability.* Jessica Kingsley, London.

Sanderson H, Kennedy J, Richie P and Goodwin G (1997) *People, Plans and Possibilities: exploring person-centred planning.* SHS, Edinburgh.

Schreiber and Libow (1993) *Hurting for Love – Munchausen by Proxy Syndrome.* Guildford Press, London.

Scott L and Kerr-Edwards L (1999) *Talking Together…about Growing Up: A Workbook for parents of children with learning disabilities.* Family Planning Association, London.

Shakespeare T and Watson D (1998) *Theoretical Perspectives on Research with Disabled Children.* In Robinson C and Stalker K (ed) *Growing up with Disability.* Jessica Kingsley, London.

Townsley R and Robinson C (1999) What rights for disabled children? Home enteral tube feeding in the community. *Children and Society.* **13**: 48–60.

Tozer R (1999) *At the Double: Supporting families with two or more severely disabled children.* National Children's Bureau, London.

Twigg J and Atkin K (1993) *Carers Percieved: Policy and Practice in Informal Care.* OU Press, Buckingham.

Ward L (1997) *Seen and Heard: Involving Disabled Children and Young People in Research and Development Projects.* York Publishing Services, York.

Westcott H (1993) *The Abuse of Disabled Children and Adults.* The NSPCC, London.

Westcott H (1994) *Abuse of children and adults who are disabled.* In French S (ed) (1994) *On Equal Terms: working with disabled people.* Butterworth Heinemann, London.

Westcott H and Cross M (1996) *This Far and no Further: Towards Ending the Abuse of Disabled Children.* Venture Press, Birmingham.

Westcott H and Jones D (1999) Annotation: The Abuse of Disabled Children. *Journal of Child Psychology and Psychiatry.* **40**(4): 497–506.

# 4

# Resources to assist effective assessment of children in need

## Introduction

4.1 This chapter provides information about practice materials, evidence based publications and training resources which were specifically commissioned by the Department of Health as part of the development of the Assessment Framework. It also includes other relevant training materials on which trainers, practitioners and managers may wish to draw. The practice materials are not comprehensive. They do not cover every aspect of the process of assessing children and families, nor every situation in which families may ask or are referred for help. The use of these materials will entail careful discrimination and thought being given to the individual circumstances of each child. They can provide checklists which may be useful for structuring what practitioners observe or discuss, and assist in the precise recording and systematic assembly of information for analysis. They complement but do not replace information gained through interviews and observations.

## The collection and recording of information

4.2 Collecting information which will help explain what is happening to children and their families and making sense of that information are key tasks in the assessment process. These tasks require knowledge, confidence and skill, underpinned by regular training and professional supervision. Materials, which help structure practitioners' thinking about the complex worlds of the families with whom they work, which assist them to record systematically and consistently what they have seen and heard, and then aid their analysis and formulation of appropriate plans, can make a significant contribution to the development of high quality work. **Good tools cannot substitute for good practice, but good practice and good tools together can achieve excellence.**

4.3 Recently many local authority social services departments have worked on new and innovative approaches for responding to referrals of children in need. Much of that work has been on finding improved ways of collecting salient information and recording it from the point of referral onwards, and producing assessment forms which reflect a broader approach to families' needs. Some of the national voluntary child care organisations, particularly those running family centres, have found imaginative ways of involving families in identifying their children's needs and distinguishing them from their own needs as parents and adults.

4.4    The **protocols, procedures, forms and methods of record keeping and practice resources** of all authorities and agencies should be consistent with the Assessment Framework and with the principles which underpin its use.

## Resources commissioned to assist the assessment process

4.5    The Department of Health commissioned a range of materials to support practice in assessment by providing ideas and increasing the repertoire of tools available to practitioners. The two main developments have been to produce a recording format to assist in the collection and analysis of information gained during an assessment of an individual child and family, and a pack of questionnaires and scales to assist assessment in particular areas, for example child wellbeing or parental mental health. These materials have been tested for their usefulness and validity with local authority and voluntary agency practitioners and managers. The assessment records will be published with the Assessment Framework and refined following further trialing and evaluation during 2000/01. The questionnaires and scales have been published in *The Family Assessment Pack of Questionnaires and Scales* (2000) which also accompanies the Assessment Framework.

## Principles underpinning the use of practice materials

4.6    The principles, summarised below, which underpin good assessment work, should be applied in the use of all questionnaires, scales and other practice materials.

---

### *PRINCIPLES FOR THE USE OF MATERIALS TO ASSIST ASSESSMENT*

**Clarity of purpose**

Clarity about aims is fundamental to all assessment. In practice these can be broad ranging or more focused, depending on timing and context, but in general there will be an intention to gather a range of relevant information in a manner that promotes or sustains a positive working relationship with those being assessed; in most circumstances information is of limited use if collaboration has broken down.

**Assessment is not a static process**

An assessment has many purposes but the process should be therapeutic. The assessment should inform the identification of current needs as well as future work, and evaluate the progress and effectiveness of interventions. The way in which the assessment is carried out is important. It should enable those involved to gain fresh perspectives on their family situation, which are in themselves helpful and assist in taking the work forward.

**Working with Children and Families is informed by professional judgement**

It follows that, although working with children and families is a fundamental principle, this does not mean that every detail on information gained, or in particular the practitioners' judgement about that information, can be shared immediately and in full with those being assessed. Sustaining working relationships and positive therapeutic impact are overriding principles and timing is therefore a consideration in deciding when and how to feed back information.

---

> **Assessment does not take place in a vacuum**
> Assessments benefit from multiple sources of information and multiple methods. Any one source used alone is likely to give either a limited or unbalanced view. This applies to all the main approaches of interviewing, observation, and the use of standardised tests and questionnaires. Limitations should be recognised. Contrasting data from different methods and/or sources are vital to developing a deeper and more balanced understanding of the child and family's situation.
>
> *From: The Family Assessment Pack of Questionnaires and Scales (2000) (see paragraph 4.14)*

## Assessment records

4.7 The Department of Health has commissioned the development of age related assessment records for use by social services front line staff when collecting, collating and analysing information gathered during an assessment of a child and family. These **assessment records of children in need and parenting capacity, within the wider family and community context** (Department of Health and Cleaver, 2000) are both research and practice based, and use the developmental dimensions of the assessment framework. They are underpinned by two important premises: that most parents want to do their best for their children; and that children can be protected from the adverse consequences of parental problems, in circumstances where another significant adult responds appropriately to the child's developmental needs.

4.8 The assessment records cannot replace professional skills, but are tools to assist social workers and other colleagues in the process of assessment, recording and decision making when undertaking an assessment. As such they are designed to help social workers record:

- the child's developmental progress;
- each caregiver's parenting capacity;
- the impact of family and environmental factors.

4.9 In order to obtain the information required to complete the assessment record, practitioners should work in an age appropriate manner, with the child and openly with the child's caregivers. Where appropriate other professionals working with the child and family, such as health workers and teachers, should be involved and their knowledge of the child and family incorporated into the record and subsequent making of judgements. The information required includes identifying the child's developmental progress, who is responding to the child's needs, and areas which should be addressed to ensure optimal outcomes for the child.

4.10 Once these domains have been explored during assessment, the format in which the information is documented on the records will help professionals analyse the child's needs and the capacity of their parents/carers to respond appropriately to those needs. This understanding should inform judgements about the child's situation and decisions about how best to help the particular child, parent(s) and other family members, for example siblings or grandparents.

4.11    The assessment records were the subject of an initial feasibility study and revision process in 1999. The records will, when used well, contribute to the achievement of greater consistency and coherence in the recording of assessments, plans of action and outcomes for children. The records will continue to be consistent with the Looking After Children Assessment and Action Records which are being revised during 1999–2001. The assessment records will be the subject of more extensive development over a two year period that will include integrating them with the Looking After Children materials. Further work will include ensuring that information gathered for children looked after who were known to the social services department prior to being looked after builds on that already recorded, thus avoiding duplication.

4.12    Information gathered about individual children, when aggregated, will assist local authority management of and planning for children's services. Further development work will be undertaken by the Department of Health, in consultation with key players, to enable salient data on individual children to be used for management information purposes, to assist both local and national planning and management of children's services. These data will also enable judgements to be made about whether the relevant Government objectives for children's social services are being met.

4.13    **A Parenting Assessment Project** which is being undertaken by North Lincolnshire Council, Home-Start and the University of Loughborough is also relevant to the assessment framework. As part of a local parenting assessment project, a process is being developed to help front line non-social services professionals, for example health visitors and teachers visiting or in contact with families, identify those parents who might need additional support in bringing up their children. Forms have been developed, on an age related basis, to help assess the level of concern about a child, the areas of child and family vulnerability and unmet need, and to assist appropriate provision of services or referral to other agencies for help. The process and forms were piloted across agencies in two areas of North Lincolnshire beginning in June 1999. Social services departments will wish to consider taking forward similar work with other agencies to facilitate appropriate referrals of children in need and joint working with vulnerable children.

## Use of questionnaires and scales in assessment

4.14    *The Family Assessment Pack of Questionnaires and Scales* (Department of Health, Cox and Bentovim, 2000) which accompany this practice guidance, contains questionnaires and scales for use by social work and other social services staff for specific purposes when undertaking assessments. It includes the following:

- Strengths and Difficulties Questionnaires;
- Parenting Daily Hassles Scale;
- Home Conditions Assessment;
- Adult Wellbeing Scale;
- Adolescent Wellbeing Scale;
- Recent Life Events Questionnaire;
- Family Activity Scales (in two age bands);
- Alcohol Scale.

4.15 There is a wide range of questionnaires and instruments available for use when assessing children and families. Those set out in paragraph 4.14 were selected because of their appropriateness for the task of undertaking assessments using the Assessment Framework and because they proved easy to incorporate into practice. The eight questionnaires and scales can be used following a process of familiarisation with the materials but do not require any formal training.

4.16 The chosen assessment instruments are concerned with child mental health and development, parental mental health, parenting capacity and the family environment. A description of each questionnaire or scale is given below (Figure 5). They are intended to assist staff undertaking assessments by providing a clear evidence base for judgements and recommendations. The use of these questionnaires and scales requires careful preparation and introduction to families by the practitioner, and a clear explanation of how they fit into an initial or core assessment. Each questionnaire or scale should be used for the purpose for which it was developed. They are intended to contribute to the overall assessment and should be applied with sensitivity and understanding.

## Figure 5  The Family Assessment Questionnaires and Scales

- **The Strengths and Difficulties Questionnaires** (Goodman et al, 1997; Goodman et al, 1998). These scales are a modification of the very widely used instruments to screen for emotional and behavioural problems in children and adolescents – the Rutter A + B scales for parents and teachers. Although similar to Rutter's, the Strengths and Difficulties Questionnaire's wording was re-framed to focus on a child's emotional and behavioural strengths as well as difficulties. The actual questionnaire incorporates five scales: pro-social, hyperactivity, emotional problems, conduct (behavioural) problems, and peer problems. In the pack, there are versions of the scale to be completed by adult caregivers, or teachers for children from age 3 to 16, and children between the ages of 11–16. These questionnaires have been used with disabled children and their teachers and carers. They are available in 40 languages on the following website: http://chp.iop.kcl.ac.uk/sdq/b3.html

- **The Parenting Daily Hassles Scale** (Crnic and Greenberg, 1990; Crnic and Booth, 1991). This scale aims to assess the frequency and intensity/impact of 20 potential parenting 'daily' hassles experienced by adults caring for children. It has been used in a wide variety of research studies concerned with children and families – particularly families with young children. It has been found that parents (or caregivers) generally like filling it out, because it touches on many aspects of being a parent that are important to them.

- **The Home Conditions Assessment** (The Family Cleanliness Scale. Davie et al, 1984) addresses various aspects of the home environment (for example, smell, state of surfaces in house, floors). The total score has been found to correlate highly with indices of the development of children.

- **Adult Wellbeing Scale** (Irritability, Depression, Anxiety – IDA Scale. Snaith et al, 1978). This scale, which was based on the Irritability, Depression and Anxiety Scale, was devised by a social worker involved in the pilot. The questions are framed in a 'personal' fashion (i.e. I feel, my appetite is…). This scale looks at how an adult is feeling in terms of their depression, anxiety and irritability. The scale allows the adult to respond from four possible answers, which enables the adult some choice, and therefore less restriction. This could enable the adult to feel more empowered.

- **The Adolescent Wellbeing Scale** (Self-rating Scale for Depression in Young People. Birleson, 1980). It was originally validated for children aged between 7–16. It involves 18 questions each relating to different aspects of a child or adolescent's life, and how they feel about these. As a result of the pilot the wording of some questions was altered in order to be more appropriate to adolescents. Although children as young as seven and eight have used it, older children's thoughts and beliefs about themselves are more stable. The scale is intended to enable practitioners to gain more insight and understanding into how an adolescent feels about their life.

- **The Recent Life Events Questionnaire** This scale was taken from Brugha et al (1985), with nine additional items added. It focuses on recent life events (ie. those occurring in the last 12 months) but could be used over a longer time-scale. It is intended to assist in the compilation of a social history. Respondents are asked to identify which of the events still affects them. It was hoped that use of the scale will:

  - result in a fuller picture of a family's history and contribute to greater contextual understanding of the family's current situation;

  - help practitioners explore how particular recent life events have affected the carer and the family;

  - in some situations, identify life events which family members have not reported earlier.

- **The Family Activity Scale** (Derived from The Child-Centredness Scale. Smith, 1985). These scales give practitioners an opportunity to explore with carers the environment provided for their children, through joint activities and support for independent activities. This includes information about the cultural and ideological environment in which children live, as well as how their carers respond to their children's actions (for example, concerning play and independence). They aim to be independent of socio-economic resources. There are two separate scales; one for children aged 2–6, and one for children aged 7–12.

- **The Alcohol Scale** This scale was developed by Piccinelli et al (1997). Alcohol abuse is estimated to be present in about 6% of primary carers, ranking it third in frequency behind major depression and generalised anxiety. Higher rates are found in certain localities, and particularly amongst those parents known to social services departments. Drinking alcohol affects different individuals in different ways. For example, some people may be relatively unaffected by the same amount of alcohol that incapacitates others. The primary concern therefore is not the amount of alcohol consumed, but how it impacts on the individual and, more particularly, on their role as a parent. This questionnaire has been found to be effective in detecting individuals with alcohol disorders and those with hazardous drinking habits.

4.17 These eight questionnaires and scales have all been well evaluated. They are widely used in psychology and psychiatry but are not commonly used in social work practice. In 1998/99 they were piloted in a number of different sites within five social services departments as part of the development of the Assessment Framework and found to be helpful.

4.18 Two other instruments, the *Home Inventory* (Caldwell and Bradley, 1984) and the *Assessment of Family Competence, Strengths and Difficulties* (Bentovim and Bingley Miller (forthcoming)) based on the Family measures described by Kinston and Loader (1984) were also piloted and practitioners found them very useful. The Home

Inventory aims to obtain a picture of what the world is like from a child's perspective and is not, therefore, exclusively focused on the care-giving activities of carers. The Assessment of Family Competence, Strengths and Difficulties provides an approach to assessing children and families which focuses on work in the following areas:

- direct assessment of the family organisation and character;

- completing a family genogram;

- undertaking family tasks;

- assessment of presenting problem/concerns and difficulties;

- exploring parents' background, childhood and developments;

- use of the family conflict tactics scale.

4.19    The pilot indicated that in order to use the above two instruments effectively, practitioners required more substantial training. The materials will be made available later in 2000 for use by practitioners and in training programmes.

4.20    Generally, these questionnaires and scales have been found to have a number of applications in practice:

- to strengthen the voice of the child or family in the assessment process;

- to clarify the nature and extent of need, either raising new issues or revealing new information during their use, or enabling practitioners to reassure families of progress;

- to provide a focus for assessment and a structure for an intervention plan;

- to provide a way of structuring discussions with families about issues the families are reluctant or feel unable to discuss;

- to provide an evidence base for reports;

- to monitor progress over time, having an open and agreed understanding between staff and families of areas in which particular changes are planned.


## Evidence based publications

4.21    The Department of Health commissioned child protection research studies, which are summarised in *Child Protection: Messages from Research* (Department of Health, 1995b), identified a number of areas where practitioners working with children and families indicated they would benefit from further exploration of the research findings. Four of these have been taken forward in publications on: child sexual abuse; parental mental illness, domestic violence, and problem alcohol and drug use; working with fathers; and communicating with children who may have been traumatised or maltreated. A fifth area identified was working with black and minority ethnic families. This has also been taken forward and is presented in chapter 2 in this publication.

4.22    Using an evidence based approach, the authors of the four publications above reviewed the available research, including relevant studies commissioned by the Department of Health, and their findings have informed the development of the

Assessment Framework. In addition these publications are intended to assist practitioners, managers and policy makers when assessing children and families and deciding which types of intervention are effective in a particular family situation.

4.23 Each publication is summarised below. Readers are encouraged to make extensive use of these publications to inform the evidence base of their work with children and families.

4.24 *Child Sexual Abuse. Informing Practice from Research* (Jones and Ramchandani, 1999) outlines the different ways in which professionals can help children who have experienced sexual abuse. It describes how professional intervention can improve the outcomes for sexually abused children and their families. The authors conclude:

- therapies can help children who have been sexually abused and those based on a cognitive-behavioural model should help the majority of children who are displaying symptoms of distress;

- treatment for children should not take place in isolation, but must include other forms of help, for example, support for the child's carers.

4.25 They suggest an algorithm (Figure 6) for helping a sexually abused child. This can be used by practitioners when deciding how best to help a child who has been sexually abused and by those planning appropriate resources for this group of children and their families.

4.26 *Children's Needs – Parenting Capacity* (Cleaver et al, 1999) addresses how parental mental illness, problem alcohol and drug misuse, and domestic violence have an impact on children's development. These potential problems affect each child differently depending on their age and circumstances. The publication focuses on children of different age groups and explores both the possible negative consequences of parenting issues and the buffering or protective factors. Practitioners can draw on this knowledge when assessing and intervening in families where there are such problems. This work underpins the assessment records under development by the Department of Health and Hedy Cleaver (see paragraphs 4.7 to 4.11).

4.27 In *Working with Fathers* (Ryan, 2000) the roles of men in contemporary society are examined and the impact of fathers on their children's development is explored. Within the general context of the role of fathers in society, findings are presented from a number of child protection studies which found that fathers were not being engaged in child and family work. Even in situations where the father was a positive and valued person in his child's life, the focus of practitioners was on mothers and children. This publication provides examples from practice on how to work with different types of fathers including those who are violent and abusive, whilst ensuring children's safety.

4.28 *Communicating with children who may have been traumatised or maltreated* (Jones, forthcoming) reviews the international literature and suggests how this knowledge can be used by practitioners in their work with children, and where there are concerns to assist children to tell their story. An important consideration is ensuring that children's communications, which may be used as evidence in criminal court processes, are appropriately managed so as not to jeopardise any legal proceedings.

# Figure 6[3]
## An Algorithm For Helping Children Who Have Been Sexually Abused

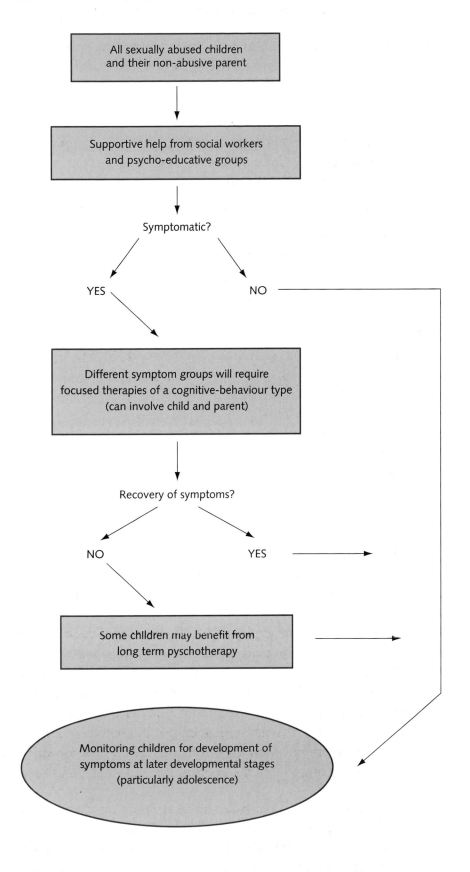

All sexually abused children
and their non-abusive parent

Supportive help from social workers
and psycho-educative groups

Symptomatic?

YES                    NO

Different symptom groups will require
focused therapies of a cognitive-behaviour type
(can involve child and parent)

Recovery of symptoms?

NO                    YES

Some children may benefit from
long term pyschotherapy

Monitoring children for development of
symptoms at later developmental stages
(particularly adolescence)

---

[3] Reproduced with kind permission from the authors of *Child Sexual Abuse: Research into Practice* (1999) Jones D P H and Ramchandani P. Radcliffe Medical Press, Abingdon.

4.29    Four studies (Department of Health, 2000) were undertaken to inform the development of the Assessment Framework. These were:

- *A review of the social work literature on assessment.* This work has made a significant contribution to the theoretical basis of the Assessment Framework. It also identifies that the theory of social work practice requires updating to take account of developments in practice over the past twenty years.

- *A study of different structures and types of assessments undertaken in a variety of settings* – social services departments, health service, voluntary agencies, family centres – which were either single agency or multi-disciplinary contexts. It suggests the type of settings, structures and cultures that facilitate assessment work.

- *A study of the language used by social workers to describe the needs of children.* A key finding was that where the Looking After Children materials were being used by social workers, they were describing the needs of children according to the seven child developmental dimensions.

- *A summary of the findings on assessment from child care inspections undertaken by the Social Services Inspectorate during the period 1993–1997.* The report identifies key messages for practitioners, managers and policy makers in relation to assessment.

4.30    These four studies provide a valuable source of information about contemporary practice and thinking. The intention is that they will inform the field, and assist in understanding the background and principles underpinning the Assessment Framework, as well as assist its implementation.

## Training resources

4.31    Training is a critical component of any strategy to implement new policy or practice and to embed it into everyday practice. To support the development of knowledge and skills, and to provide learning opportunities for practitioners to become familiar with the Assessment Framework and associated practice materials, a training pack has been developed concurrently with the Guidance. This pack has been designed to be used also in future training on the Assessment Framework and to be adapted for a variety of training purposes. Selected training resources either commissioned by or produced with the Department of Health have also been identified to help practitioners with some of the specific issues which may arise when undertaking a child and family assessment.

4.32    *The Child's World: Assessing Children in Need. Training and Development Pack* was commissioned by the Department of Health and produced by the NSPCC and the University of Sheffield (2000). It consists of:

- **A Video** of trigger material highlighting issues about assessment in a variety of different circumstances. The material is presented in six scenarios, covering different aspects of assessment practice, and by children and young people including disabled young people, describing their experiences of assessment. The scenarios focus on planning the initial stages of an initial or core assessment but can be used for all stages in the process.

- **A Training Guide** which provides trainers with activities, materials and guidance to facilitate learning for a range of different audiences, although primarily aimed at social services staff. It includes four modules:

  - Introduction to the Assessment Framework;

  - The process of assessment;

  - Assessing children's developmental needs within their family and environmental context;

  - Assessing parenting capacity to respond to their child's developmental needs within their environmental context.

- **A Reader** designed to provide practitioners, front-line managers and trainers with an overview of theory, research and practice developments relevant to assessing children in need and their families. The Reader consists of four modules:

  - The framework: background and context;

  - The assessment process: the task for practitioners and their supervisors;

  - The developmental needs of children: research, theory and practice implications;

  - Parenting capacity: factors that impact on carers ability to respond appropriately to the needs of children in their care.

4.33   The Reader can be purchased separately from the rest of the Pack (Horwath (ed), 2000). It is a valuable source of reference for those using the Assessment Framework, and provides a route to further study of contemporary theory and research by practitioners and their managers.

4.34   The objectives of the training and development pack are to provide trainers with resources to:

- support the implementation and use of the Guidance on assessing children in need and their families;

- support the implementation and continuing understanding of *Working Together to Safeguard Children* (1999) in relation to the assessment of children where there are concerns about significant harm;

- enable practitioners and managers to become familiar with the Assessment Framework and to develop the necessary knowledge, skills and attitudes to use the framework in practice;

- provide learning opportunities to improve the quality of assessments and outcomes for children in need;

- enable practitioners and managers to use the framework in the context of national and local policies and resources;

- provide a link between training based on this material and relevant qualifying and post qualifying awards.

4.35   Key texts and articles as well as training programmes are also highlighted in the directory *Undertaking Assessments of Children And Families* (Connolly and Shemmings, 1998). This publication was commissioned by the Department of Health as a resource for those involved in training and for use by individuals who may wish to pursue their own independent professional learning. The directory of training materials, key texts and programmes is divided into seven sections, covering respectively the areas of Training Packs, Videos, Open Learning Materials, Computer-based Information Services, Key Texts and Articles, Post-Qualifying Courses and NVQ Based Learning Opportunities. It describes the materials briefly in order to help the reader decide which materials will be helpful for the purpose, but does not evaluate them. It is a comprehensive source of reference to inform planning the implementation and use of this Guidance through training and continuing professional development.

4.36 Two training packs were commissioned by the Department of Health to assist staff working in both adult and children's services to ensure that children's development will not be adversely affected when their parents have problems with mental illness or domestic violence respectively. They complement Cleaver et al's publication *Children's Needs – Parenting Capacity* (1999).

## Parental Mental Health

*Crossing Bridges – Training resources for working with mentally ill parents and their children (1998)* It contains a reader for managers, practitioners and trainers which in turn introduces and supports the associated training materials. Information is provided on:

- key topics in adult mental health

- parenting and parent–child relationships

- child development and mental health

- legislation

- implications for practice

## Domestic Violence

*Making an Impact. Children and Domestic Violence* (1998)
This pack also contains a reader and training pack which have been designed to ensure ready availability of training for front line staff dealing with domestic violence.

4.37 A third training pack, to be published later in 2000, has been commissioned by the Department of Health to assist adult and children's services staff work together. It's focus is on working with physically disabled parents and their children, assessing their needs and providing appropriate services.

4.38 Five further training packs, which the Department of Health either commissioned or was closely involved in their development, are also relevant to practitioners. They address a number of key areas relating to the Assessment Framework. The contents of these are set out below.

## Direct work with children

*Turning Points: A Resource Pack for Communicating with Children* (1997)
NSPCC in association with Chailey Heritage, with support of the Department
of Health.

This pack promotes a child-centred approach to working with children and
young people, including those who are disabled. It builds on the principles of the
Children Act 1989 and endorses Article 12 of the United Nations Convention
on the Rights of the Child, placing emphasis on the rights of children not only to
be protected, but also to have their voice heard.

## Involving young people in the process of assessment

*In on the Act – A Training Programme for Relevant Professionals* (1999)
Shemmings D, School of Social Work, University of East Anglia.

The programme has four main aims:

- To raise participants' awareness of key dilemmas for practitioners when
increasing the involvement of children in family support and child protection;
- To offer professionals taking part the chance to explore new ways of involving
children in decision-making;
- To give participants an opportunity to improve their skills by considering
practical examples from the fields of family support and child protection;
- To help professionals discuss the options and consequences of different
outcomes when children are consulted about decisions which affect their lives.

## Family Decision Making

*Family Group Conferences: A Training Pack* (1998) Morris K, Marsh P, and
Wiffen J, The Family Rights Group, London

The Pack contains background information about Family Group Conferences
and contains a number of exercises which addresses the following areas:

- The Family Group Conference model
- The context for Family Group Conferences
- Attitudes to families and a consideration of the need for change
- Skills development
- Local knowledge

## Working with separated children and young people living outside their Country of origin

*Unaccompanied Asylum-Seeking Children: A Training Pack* (1995) Social Services
Inspectorate, Department of Health and Surrey County Council. This pack
contains practice guidance and information about relevant resources. It pays
particular attention to sensitive issues for consideration when assessing children
in these circumstances.

### Assessing the progress of looked after children

- *Looking After Children: Training Resource Pack* (1995a) Department of Health. It contains a comprehensive set of materials which can be used flexibly to support up to two days of training for social workers, foster carers, residential workers, students and others who have some responsibility for looking after children. It comprises:

- **Management and Implementation Guide** This contains key information for managers and supervisors about organisational and practice issues.

- **Training Guide** Contains introductory materials, guidance on setting up a training programme, sample training programmes with workshops, reading materials, learning exercises, case examples and other resources to support staff training and development.

- **Training Video** A 50-minute VHS tape, which shows the Assessment and Action Records being used by social workers and foster carers with six children and young people and their families. Inter-agency aspects of this work are also highlighted.

- **Video Notes** A book containing notes about the video and its use in training.

- **Reader** This contains short papers which address the concepts and philosophy supporting the Looking After Children materials; the developmental dimensions; and practice issues.

- **Demonstration Documents** Two complete sets of Looking After Children documents.

4.39 Two publications *Adoption Now: Messages from Research* (Department of Health, 1999) and the *The Children Act 1989 Now: Messages from Research* (Department of Health, forthcoming) summarise major Department of Health commissioned studies on Adoption and the Children Act 1989 respectively. These are important resources for improving practice in work with children and families.

4.40 The materials should be used extensively and imaginatively in qualifying training, continuing study and private learning by all those with responsibility for work with children and families. Of critical importance is keeping up to date to ensure a sound basis of knowledge for evidence based practice.

# References – Chapter 4

Bentovim A and Bingley Miller L (forthcoming) *Assessment of Family Competence, Strengths and Difficulties.*

Birleson P (1980) The validity of depressive disorder in childhood and the development of a self-rating scale: A research report. *Journal of Child Psychology and Psychiatry.* **22:** 73–88.

Brugha T, Bebington P, Tennant C and Hurry J (1985) The list of threatening experiences: A subset of 12 life event categories with considerable long-term contextual threat. *Psychological Medicine.* **15:** 189–194.

Caldwell B M and Bradley R H (1984) *Home Observation for Measurement of the Environment – Administration Manual (revised edition).* University of Arkansas, Arkansas.

Cleaver H, Unell I and Aldgate J (1999) *Children's Needs – Parenting Capacity: The impact of parental mental illness, problem alcohol and drug use, and domestic violence on children's development.* The Stationery Office, London.

*Code of Practice for the Disability Discrimination Rights of Access – Goods, Facilities, Services and Premises.* The Stationery Office, London.

Connolly J and Shemmings D (1998) *Undertaking Assessments of Children and Families: A directory of training materials, courses and key texts.* University of East Anglia, Norwich.

*Crime and Disorder Act 1998* (1998) The Stationery Office, London.

Crnic K A & Greenberg M T (1990) Minor parenting stresses with young children. *Child Development.* **61:** 1628–1637.

Crnic K A & Booth C L (1991) Mothers' and fathers' perceptions of daily hassles of parenting across early childhood. *Journal of Marriage and the Family.* **53:** 1043–1050.

Davie C E, Hutt S J, Vincent E and Mason M (1984) *The young child at home.* NFER-Nelson, Windsor.

Department of Health (1995a) *Looking After Children: Training Pack.* HMSO, London.

Department of Health (1995b) *Child Protection: Messages from Research.* HMSO, London.

Department of Health (1999) *Adoption Now: Messages from Inspection.* Wiley, Chichester.

Department of Health (2000) *Studies which inform the development of the Framework for the Assessment of Children in Need and their Families.* The Stationery Office, London.

Department of Health (forthcoming) *The Children Act 1989 Now: Messages from Research.* The Stationery Office, London.

Department of Health and Cleaver H (2000) *Assessment Recording Forms.* The Stationery Office, London.

Department of Health, Cox A and Bentovim A (2000) *The Family Assessment Pack of Questionnaires and Scales.* The Stationery Office, London.

Department of Health, Home Office, Department for Education and Employment (1999) *Working Together to Safeguard Children: A guide to inter-agency working to safeguard and promote the welfare of children.* The Stationery Office, London.

Department of Health, University of Bristol, the NSPCC and Barnardos (1998) *Making an Impact: Children and Domestic Violence: Training Resource.* Barnardos, London.

Falkov A, Mayes K, Diggins M, Silverdale N, and Cox A (1998) *Crossing Bridges – Training resources for working with mentally ill parents and their children.* Pavilion Publishing, Brighton.

Goodman R (1997) The Strengths and Difficulties Questionnaire: A Research Note. *Journal of Child Psychology and Psychiatry.* **38**: 581–586.

Goodman R, Meltzer H and Bailey V (1998) The strengths and difficulties questionnaire: A pilot study on the validity of the self-report version. *European Child and Adolescent Psychiatry.* **7**: 125–130.

Horwath J. (ed) (2000) *The Child's World: Assessing Children in Need. The Reader.* The NSPCC, London.

Jones D and Ramchandani P (1999) *Child Sexual Abuse: Informing Practice from Research.* Radcliffe Medical Press. Abingdon.

Jones D P H (forthcoming) *Communicating with children who may have been traumatised or maltreated (working title).*

Kinston W and Loader P (1988) The Family Task Interview: A tool for clinical research in family interaction. *Journal of Marital and Family Therapy.* **14**: 67–87.

Marsh P and Peel M (1999) *Leaving Care in Partnership: family involvement with care leavers.* The Stationery Office, London.

Morris K, Marsh P and Wiffin J (1998) *Family Group Conferences – A Training Pack.* The Family Rights Group, London.

The NSPCC in association with Chailey Heritage and Department of Health (1997) *Turning Points: A Resource Pack for Communicating with Children.* The NSPCC, London.

The NSPCC and the University of Sheffield (2000) *The Child's World: Assessing Children in Need. Training and Development Pack.* The NSPCC, London.

Piccinelli M, Tessari E, Bortolomasi M, Piasere O, Semenzin M, Garzotto N and Tansella M (1997) Efficacy of the alcohol use disorders identification test as a screening tool for hazardous alcohol intake and related disorders in primary care: A validity study. *British Medical Journal.* **514**: 420–424.

Ryan M (2000) *Working with Fathers.* Radcliffe Medical Press, Abingdon.

Shemmings D (1999) *In on the Act – A Training Programme for Relevant Professionals. School of Social Work*, University of East Anglia, Norwich.

Smith M A (1985) *The Effects of Low Levels of Lead on Urban Children: The relevance of social factors.* Ph.D. Psychology, University of London.

Snaith R P, Constantopoulos A A, Jardine M Y and McGuffin P (1978) A clinical scale for the self-assessment of irritability. *British Journal of Psychiatry.* **132**: 164–171.

Social Services Inspectorate and Surrey County Council (1995) *Unaccompanied Asylum-Seeking Children: A Training Pack.* Department of Health, London.